A Stroke of Faith

A Stroke of Faith

A Stroke Survivor's Story of a Second Chance
at Living a Life of Significance

Mark Moore
with Andy Butcher

NEW YORK NASHVILLE

FaithWords
Hachette Book Group
1290 Avenue of the Americas, New York, NY 10104
faithwords.com
twitter.com/faithwords

First Edition: April 2017

FaithWords is a division of Hachette Book Group, Inc. The FaithWords name and logo are trademarks of Hachette Book Group, Inc.

The publisher is not responsible for websites (or their content) that are not owned by the publisher.

The Hachette Speakers Bureau provides a wide range of authors for speaking events. To find out more, go to www.hachettespeakersbureau.com or call (866) 376-6591.

LCCN: 2017930390

ISBNs: 978-1-4555-7111-6 (hardcover), 978-1-4555-7110-9 (ebook)

Printed in the United States of America

LSC-C

10   9   8   7   6   5   4   3   2   1

To God the great three-in-one: the Father, Jesus Christ His only Son, and the Holy Spirit: You are the only reason there is a story to tell, because of Your love and mercy.

To my parents, James and Lollie Moore, and "second dad and mom," George and Louise Moore: You helped me to believe I could achieve, through your example and encouragement.

To Brenda, my bride and best friend: You continue to inspire and delight me every day with your love; I wouldn't be here without you.

To my children: Jenée and Markus, and "second son" Gerald: You bring me joy as I watch you pursue your own dreams.

To stroke survivors everywhere: You have a story of your own to write! I hope mine may encourage you on your journey.

CONTENTS

CONTENTS

FOREWORD

"It's not about me," Mark protested emphatically as I talked with him about his experience in overcoming two strokes and fighting back to carry on a normal life. You see, Mark wanted everyone to know that his recovery was the act of a sovereign God, or the work of gifted physicians, therapists, nurses, and other caregivers, or due to the extensive network of family and friends who supported him throughout the long road to recovery. He did not want any of the credit for his near-miraculous recovery and restoration of a normal life.

As the CEO of a large, sophisticated health system, I know patients often attribute their recovery to the skill and dedication of extraordinary surgeons, physicians, and allied health professionals. In fact, the wonders of modern science that restore health to patients suffering from life-threatening illness or accident are becoming increasingly common. In truth, the billions of dollars spent each year on research into the causes of illness and the best ways to treat it lead many patients and doctors alike to worship at the altar of science.

In healthcare, the truth is we know that science explains many of the mysteries of this life. In the hands of a well-trained doctor and her team, science becomes the agent of healing that saves so many from death, not to mention tremendous suffering and disability. At the same time, we know that patients often think that their physician is the agent of God's will in their lives.

They conclude that God directed their care and/or the presence of crucial caregivers who intervene at just the right, lifesaving moment. At the same time, the question remains of why they survived a near-death experience, and they often think initially about the role the Almighty must have played.

As recovery proceeds and the perilous hours pass into further recesses of their memory, patients usually then begin to see the role they themselves play in the process of achieving recovery and rehabilitation. The hard work of physical rehabilitation especially, often grueling and painful, leaves them dripping with perspiration and exhausted from the extreme exertion.

Progress is slow and sometimes invisible on a day-to-day basis. Many, if not most, patients become discouraged and accept their new loss of capacity and function. They *want* to reclaim their old life but have lost the will to endure the daily pain. Simply put, they have lost hope that they can make it back.

When he first awoke from his coma, Mark Moore was not able to move his head. He could not raise his arms or move his legs. His only form of communication was to blink his eyes "yes" or "no" in response to questions. Initially, he was totally dependent upon others for the most basic of human functions—eating, toileting, turning, and positioning so he could breathe without assistance. He was dependent upon his caregivers for everything—for his life and for his prospect even for survival.

Experienced caregivers know that it is typically at this point that hope must be "transplanted" into a patient if they are to regain their sense of self and the desire to recover. Mark, however, did not really need a transplant of hope. When Brenda, his wife, first explained what had happened to him, how he had been in a coma for almost a month, he told her, "I have got to get out of this bed." When nothing happened as he tried to move the various parts of his body, he looked back at her in a way that signaled his determination to find out what he had to do to turn his life toward the goals of recovery.

Mark wanted to get well and he was ready to do whatever it took to make it happen. He told the physical therapists who came to treat him to give him whatever hard work they wanted to throw at him. He could take the pain, he said—he could and would do whatever it took to get back. Unfortunately, it rapidly became clear that his recovery was not up to just him; it was up to all those therapists and doctors who were in total control of his life.

It became clear that Mark had to surrender his will to theirs, and in doing so, he took perhaps the most important step in his recovery. He knew from his foundation in the Christian faith that he had to surrender to a higher power to claim the life he wished to live with Brenda and his family.

In this book, Mark tells of an extraordinary chapter in his life that was not of his own making. Some of the story is written by God and by the science of the genetics that brought about Mark's strokes and his response to his first collapse. Some of the story is written by the incredible physicians, nurses, therapists, and other health professionals who set to work using the best that science had to offer to bring about the restoration of a purposeful, impactful life. Some of the story is written by Brenda, who built and decorated the infrastructure of human support without which nothing else would have worked.

It is a story of miracles, of a life that was reclaimed by miracles wrought by healthcare workers and by the Almighty. It is a story that teaches us our part in miracles, and how those who find themselves in a similar place can find a road to recovery that will please both God and man.

Read and learn.

Knox Singleton
Chief Executive Officer
Inova Health System
Falls Church, Virginia
July 2016

A Stroke of Faith

INTRODUCTION
"BEYOND MY CONTROL!"

We all have gifts of one kind or another, natural abilities that seem to flow out of the very core of who we are. For some, it's music. They can look at a sheet of music and hear the melody in their heads as if a full symphony orchestra were playing right in front of them. Others have a knack for languages. A few lessons, and they sound like native speakers.

I was always a numbers man. Math may not be as glamorous as melodies and words, but I never saw just a bunch of figures on a page. For me, they turned into a score or a story I could follow. A company spreadsheet could be like an X-ray, revealing all the inner problems of an ailing business. Or it might become a road map, pointing the way to prosperity. I could read columns of debits and credits like a book.

As with any innate ability, that aptitude could take me only so far. Raw sugarcane has to go through a process to release the sweetness. With application and determination, I was able to harness my gift for math in ways that transformed my life. It took me from a tough New York City borough to the leafy suburbs of Washington, DC. From a two-bedroom house into which ten of us were squeezed to a ten-thousand-square-foot property with a pool.

During that climb up the ladder of success, I had raised two billion dollars in capital as I rode the financial wave of twenty-first-century new technology. Overcoming some preju- dice along the way, as one of a minority of successful African American entrepreneurs, I'd established a reputation as a fair but firm businessman.

Proud to be a self-made man who had a different, tailor- made suit to wear for every day of the month—a far cry from the hand-me-down wardrobe of my childhood—I had written more checks than I could remember, the largest single one for a half million dollars.

And now I stared helplessly at the blank check that Lisa had placed in front of me. I could read the words: *Pay to the Bearer* and all that. I could see the lines and the blank box where I was supposed to write the payee's name and the amount.

But I didn't know how to do it. Something was missing between what I knew in my brain and the pen I held in my right hand. It was like one of the bulbs had shorted out midway in a string of Christmas lights, breaking the connection and extin- guishing them all. The chain was interrupted.

I should have known without even thinking what needed to be done, but somehow I just could not bring to mind the steps necessary for completing the simple actions I had performed so many times previously. I froze, mentally paralyzed.

Here I was, the successful numbers man, and I could not even put two and two together.

I felt crushed, helpless. The head-down determination that had brought so many rewards was somewhere out of reach. No matter how much I gritted my teeth and concentrated, I just could not will myself to do something as basic as writing a check.

To make matters worse, I could not even spring up and pace about in frustration. A lifelong athlete, I had pushed myself as hard on the basketball court in my two-hour weekly games as I had in my twelve-hour days at the office. A nonsmoking nondrinker, I was in excellent shape for a man in his midforties.

But now I could only sit in my wheelchair as I contemplated the chasm between what my life had been and what it was now— and might be for as long as I was alive.

That I was even breathing was something of a miracle itself. A month or so earlier I had been within minutes of dying, my life saved only by emergency surgery that opened up my skull and left me in a medically induced coma. I had, of course, been grateful to open my eyes again and see my beloved wife, Brenda, and our two children. But facing the rest of my life as a shadow of who I had been weighed heavily on me now.

Overwhelmed by not being able to manage such a rudimentary action, one I had performed so many times previously, I sighed.

"This is crazy," I said. "Something so simple I've done it a million times, and yet it's beyond my control!"

Sensing my discouragement, Lisa smiled brightly at me as we sat in her speech therapist's office at Mount Vernon Hospital in Alexandria, Virginia. Petite, with dark curly hair, dressed in hospital scrubs and sneakers, she managed to sound professional and personable at the same time.

"The brain is really quite remarkable in the way it can recover from a traumatic injury like the one you have suffered, Mark," she told me. "You are going to get better. Most of the progress in recovery usually occurs in the first year or two. And we are going to do all that we can to help."

Though the gap between my former life and my present circumstances seemed vast, miles wide, I had been brought to its edge by something quite small: a ruptured blood vessel deep in my brain.

Two strokes had pulled the curtain down firmly on the first act of my life. How the rest of my story would unfold was unclear and, for the first time that I could remember, seemed beyond my control.

CHAPTER 1

"EVERYTHING SEEMS FINE"

There are days when you know life is going to be different from that point on. When you walk across the stage at graduation. When you walk down the aisle at your wedding. When you walk from the cemetery after your mother's funeral. I had experienced all three.

And then there are days when life takes a completely unexpected turn, when everything flips in a moment. Like May 12, 2007, when I walked across the grass at Brown's Chapel Park.

It had been about a ten-minute drive to afternoon baseball practice for my son, Markus, and me from our home in Oak Hill, a pleasant suburban community in Virginia's Fairfax County. Markus shared my passion for sports and I loved that he was following in my footsteps by playing, even as his strides were getting longer than mine—at fifteen he was already starting to outgrow me.

I'd been helping coach the Rockies, the rec team on which he played outfield, for a couple of years. I still worked long hours at the office, as I had throughout my career, but I'd been making some changes recently. Aware of having missed too many of Markus's older sister Jenée's high school track meets, I had begun to carve out some time to be more involved with him.

It was a beautiful day, if a little unseasonably warm. We were walking an inclined field to the baseball diamond from the parking lot when I realized something was a bit off. I began to lose some of my sense of balance, and it took all my concentration to walk in a straight line and not veer off to the left.

As I felt my pulse rise, all I could think was, *Focus, Mark. Walk straight! You don't want the other parents to think you have been drinking!*

I had been drunk only once in my life, but I recognized the same uncomfortable sense of slight detachment from my movements, the need to be deliberate about each step I took.

"Hold up, son," I called to Markus as I dropped down on one knee. "Just need to check my cleats." Perhaps this sense of imbalance would clear if I just took a short time-out. I made a slow show of retying the knot in my right shoe, then switching legs and doing the other.

Standing up, I still didn't feel quite right, but I made it over to the dugout and greeted Carlos, the head coach, and everyone else. I didn't mention my dizziness to anyone, hoping it would just pass off.

And it seemed to, at least for the next couple of hours. Carlos had me work with some of the kids in groups, first on pitching practice, then on infield practice. I showed them how to make a base pass and hit some balls for them to field.

It was around four thirty p.m. by the time we wrapped practice up, and I felt pretty good. *Must have just passed off, whatever that was,* I thought. But then it came back with a vengeance as Markus and I walked back across the field to the car.

There's a relay game people play where the runners get to one end of the course and then have to put their forehead down on top of a stick standing vertically on the ground and circle around several times before sprinting back the way they came. Those spins affect their balance, and they end up running off at crazy angles, falling over as the spectators laugh. That was kind of how I felt; everything was lurching off to my left side.

The next day was Mother's Day, and the park was just down the road from North Point Village Center, where there was a Hall-mark store. So when we got into my Mercedes, I turned to Markus in the passenger seat. "Hey, Marky, let's run over to the store so you can choose a card for your mother. I've chosen one for you up to now, but you're old enough to select your own this year."

I kept my tone low-key, not wanting to alarm Markus in any way, as I added, "And I may want to call your mother to come get us from there, okay? I'm not feeling so great."

I managed the short drive to the store without any problems, but whatever was going on got worse once I was out of the car again. I felt so unsteady that I asked Markus to come and stand on my left side, so he could help me if I should fall. He seemed a little concerned, but I continued to try to downplay the situation.

By the time Markus had chosen a card and we had paid, the wobbliness was more pronounced. And now I was losing the sensation in my left side. My arm felt like lead.

Outside the store I had to stop. "Markus," I said, pulling some money from my pocket, "go buy me a bottle of water, would you?" I'd not drunk any water during the practice; maybe I was a bit dehydrated.

I chugged a few mouthfuls down when he came back, pouring more over my head. I was losing the sensation in my left leg by now as well, but I managed to pull my flip phone out of my pocket with my right hand.

"Son, I need you to call your mother," I said. "I'm not able to drive us home."

Things were getting pretty fuzzy.

"Bren," I told her, "I'm not feeling well. I need you to come and get Markus."

I could sense the concern in her voice when she asked what was wrong, and I tried to explain. In all our years together, she had never known me to miss a day's work from sickness. Even two separate Achilles heel surgeries hadn't kept me in the hospital overnight; both times I'd gone home later that same day, even been back at my desk the next morning.

But Brenda's nursing training kicked in and she remained calm as she asked what my symptoms were. I did my best to answer her questions clearly, even as I felt myself draining away inside.

"Do you need me to come and take you to the hospital?" she asked.

"No," I answered. "Come get Markus, but call an ambulance now, please." I sat down on the edge of a raised flower bed, then slid down to the ground with my back against the flower bed wall, before slowly slumping over onto my side.

Having lost sensation in my left hand, I could not close my flip phone, so I handed it to Markus, who tried to explain to his mom what was going on. I was vaguely aware of people passing by, a couple of them asking if I was okay. Despite the way things were blurring, I thought, *Well, that's a pretty dumb question.*

Then there was the sound of sirens, and soon two paramedics were kneeling down beside me.

"Can you get up?"

They asked other questions—my name, where I lived, what

I'd been doing, who was with me—to try to gauge what was wrong. When I mentioned the baseball practice, one of them asked when I had last had something to eat or drink.

"This morning."

"Hmm," he said. "Well you're probably just a bit dehydrated. We're going to get you set up here with an IV and some fluids, and you should be fine pretty soon."

It was reassuring to see over their shoulders that Brenda had arrived and was with Markus; I had been concerned that this whole thing must be a bit worrying for him. He'd never seen me incapacitated in any way before.

Once I had been lifted into the back of the ambulance on a stretcher, one of the crew stuck a needle into a vein in my forearm. The saline solution should have almost immediately eased my suspected dehydration symptoms, but instead it made me violently nauseous. As the paramedic reached for a bucket for me, his colleague hit the emergency lights and headed off for the nearest ER, at Reston Hospital.

As I lay there, feeling sick and numb, I thought, *I hope this isn't a stroke...*

I had heard the word in relation to my own health for the first time only a few days earlier. Until then, as far as I was concerned, strokes were something that happened to old people or to folks who didn't take good care of themselves.

That ruled me out on both counts. At forty-six, I still considered myself to be in the prime of life. Up at five a.m. every day, even on the weekends. Long days with lots of pressure, but I never felt stressed-out. Rather, it was an adrenaline rush: every obstacle or setback was a challenge to be overcome by working harder and longer.

I applied the same technique on the basketball court. At five feet seven inches, I gave up height to most of the other players, but I closed the gap by extra hustle. Despite surgery on both heels through the years, I hadn't lost any pace or spring.

Other than as a visitor, the only time I had been in the hospital personally was for the day-patient repairs of my basketball injuries. I made sure to have all my regular health checkups, and I was always given a clean bill of health.

Mom had died of breast cancer when I was a teenager, and Dad had heart problems later in life, but there was no general family history of serious sickness. And while I wasn't superpicky about my diet, Brenda and I made sure that we ate fairly healthily.

With no real history of ill health, I had been completely surprised by the headaches that had begun a few months earlier. I was in a meeting at work around the first week of January when, out of nowhere, my head began pounding. My vision flickered and stuttered, as though a computer screen was flashing on and off in front of me. There was an intense pain somewhere in the back of my head.

It was so bad that I couldn't concentrate on what the person sitting in my office, one of ten direct reports, was saying. I put out a hand, "Excuse me, just a moment, can you stop for a second? I'm having this bad migraine. Give me a minute and let's see if it goes away."

Sure enough, the pain faded and I was able to pick up the conversation. I shook it off. But the incident surprised me enough that I mentioned it to Brenda when I got home.

She knew something about migraines from her nursing and her own personal experience—she'd suffered from them herself at various times. On occasion they would force her to retreat to a darkened room and take medication to ease them.

Brenda asked a few questions about what had happened, and then we both pretty much forgot about it—until the following week. There I was in another direct-report meeting, and the same thing happened again. Blinding pain and short-circuited vision for a minute or so; then the storm passed.

This time it got a little bit more of our attention. Brenda wondered whether it might be stress—business was booming, so my already full days were getting fuller—but suggested I make an appointment with our family doctor, Dr. John Phillips.

He ran a battery of tests. He checked my blood pressure, looked into my eyes, and took various samples. That flashing in my vision, he said, was an "aura." "But I don't know what's causing the migraine," he told me. "From what I can tell here, everything seems fine."

The headaches might be connected to some recent dental surgery I'd had, he suggested. But he did recommend I see a neurologist, who went a little deeper. He arranged for me to have an MRI to check for a tumor, and an MRA to investigate the state of my blood vessels. Both were clear. This round of appointments played out over a few weeks, during which time the migraines continued in their intermittent, here-and-gone fashion.

Then one came on a Friday evening, when we had a friend over to visit. It grew so strong I had to excuse myself and lie down on our bed. I took some aspirin and slept fitfully, but the pain persisted. By late afternoon the following day, Brenda was concerned.

"Come on, we are taking you to the emergency room," she said.

We started to get ready and then, suddenly, it was gone. The pain washed away, like sunshine after dark clouds and rain. I felt so much better.

"I really want to take you to the ER, but there's no point now because they aren't going to be able to see anything," Brenda said. "But you have to go back to the doctor."

The neurologist checked me out again but remained baffled. He sent me to another neurologist, to get a second opinion. This doctor looked at all the films of my old tests and then ran a series of his own.

"Well, Mark, I've taken a thorough look at everything, and I cannot see any indication why you're experiencing these migraines," he told me.

I was relieved to hear that there was nothing obviously, seriously wrong, but at the same time I was a little concerned. There might be no apparent cause, but I was certainly suffering from the effects of these attacks!

"Here's what I am going to suggest," the neurologist went on calmly. "I am so confident that there is nothing to worry about here that I am going to suggest that you just go home. Let's give it another three months. If you're still having them then, come back and we can talk about whether we want to do some exploratory surgery to find out what's going on."

Exploratory surgery? That sounds kind of serious, I thought as he continued. "But I have to be honest with you, Mark." he said. "That's not something to contemplate lightly. This kind of surgery is quite delicate, and there is some risk of it causing a stroke."

That really got my attention. *Stroke?* That sounded even more serious.

I was a little concerned now, but even more frustrated; it had been several months and we had not yet found out what was causing these migraines. We'd been to two experts and had a series of tests and still no one was the wiser. How could this be?

Brenda tried to explain that sometimes, when it came to

health issues, life wasn't always black and white. Things could happen with no apparent cause, no rhyme or reason, she said. But that wasn't very satisfying to me. I was used to everything having an answer; in accounting there was always a bottom line. Why not in medicine?

Nevertheless, we both felt that we were in the best medical hands possible, so we would trust their judgment and see how things went over the next couple of months or so.

Two days after my let's-wait-and-see consultation with neurologist number two, I sweated out another Thursday night basketball game. And two days after that I found myself being rushed to the hospital in the back of an ambulance, remembering the word *stroke*.

The pain began on the short, five-minute ride to the hospital. Sharp, stabbing flares of bright hurt in the center of my head, wave after wave. It felt like my brain was going to burst.

The pain made me gasp, almost taking my breath away. I'd always had a high threshold for discomfort, having been taught growing up in a home where money was tight not to make an undue fuss. I learned to just double down and push through. I'd tried to foster the same kind of attitude in my kids. When Markus was finding it hard going at practice or in a game, I would encourage him to keep going. "Remember, you're hurting, not injured," I would tell him.

Both times I'd ruptured my Achilles playing basketball I'd driven myself home and popped a couple of Tylenol before going to the doctor the next day. But this pain was of a whole different magnitude.

By the time we arrived at Reston Hospital I was curled up on my side in a fetal position, my hands gripping my head as though to hold it together in one piece and prevent it from exploding. I groaned and groaned.

Brenda arrived right behind the ambulance and accompanied me as I was wheeled into an emergency bay. "This really hurts, Bren," I told her through gritted teeth.

A nurse came by and I asked her to give me something for the pain. She said that she couldn't do that yet because they needed to run some tests first and didn't want any medications to compromise the results.

Normally I am a pretty easygoing guy, even in pressure situations: I find being calm and collected tends to work better than getting wound up. But the unrelenting pain was too much.

"I understand that, Nurse," I said, trying to sound reasonable. "So when is the doctor going to get here?"

The nurse told me that she didn't know.

"Well, that's a problem," I said, getting testy. "If you can tell me he's going to be here in, say, two minutes, then I can wait two minutes. But we've been waiting half an hour now already, and if you tell me we are going to have to wait for another thirty minutes, there's just no way I can do that. This is too bad. I need something to stop it hurting. Now."

Thankfully, the doctor arrived and completed his examination so I could be given a painkiller. I swallowed the two tablets with a cup of water, and soon the pulsing pain began to ebb away. So did I; everything started to drift in and out as the meds took their effect. There would be soothing peace, and then briefly I'd be aware of Brenda somewhere in the room to which I had been moved.

When I came to sometime later, it was morning and I was momentarily confused. I remembered collapsing outside the

Hallmark store, the ambulance, the hospital. And the pain—
which now, mercifully, was gone. It was so good to be free of
that intense pressure in my head. And I had sensation in my left
arm and leg again. I could move my left hand and fingers. Relief
swept over me.

Then, as I blinked and focused, I saw them standing in a
huddle near my bed. A group of people, looking concerned:
Brenda and her sister, Michele, with her husband, Clarence,
and several of my siblings—Rochelle, Joanne, Sharon, Donna,
and Greg.

They all live in New York City, I thought.

"What are you all doing here?" I asked.

"Brenda called yesterday, so we came right away," Rochelle
said.

I was touched but at the same time a bit embarrassed at being
the center of such concern. We didn't know what was wrong with
me; I might just have an upset stomach or some strange bug, for
goodness' sake. Maybe this was a lot of fuss about nothing.

A doctor came in before we could talk more, ushering everyone out except for Brenda. Then he turned to us both.

"How are you feeling this morning, Mr. Moore?"

"Okay, I think. Good, thanks. The headache has gone. What
happened to me?"

"We think you might have had a mini-stroke," the doctor
said.

That *stroke* word again. Perhaps he saw my eyes go a bit wide,
because he made a sort of dismissive gesture. "Actually, we call
it a TIA—a transient ischemic attack," he went on. "It's not an
actual stroke, per se; it's more like a warning sign. The blood
flow to part of your brain gets blocked for just a short time,

maybe because of a blood clot. But then it passes, and the blood starts flowing again."

His matter-of-fact tone was somewhat reassuring. "We think you are going to be just fine," he went on. "We want to keep you here and observe you for a couple of days, just to make sure everything is okay, but we don't think it is anything to worry about."

His words were comforting and troubling at the same time. I liked the "mini" part; that didn't sound too serious. But the "stroke" bit wasn't very encouraging. All I could think of was how people who had suffered a stroke were left incapacitated, sitting in wheelchairs, unable to speak clearly, even drooling.

The doctor stayed only a few minutes. I took that as a good sign too, in an odd way; if things were serious, surely he would spend more time with me, explaining more. When he left, the rest of my family came back into the room.

"So what did the doctor have to say?" someone asked.

"He says that I've had a mini-stroke," I told them. Tears welled up in my eyes as I spoke the words, spilling from some-where unexpected. I was surprised by this flash of emotion. Tears didn't come to me readily; the last time my family had seen me cry was at a funeral—for Mom, for Dad, and for our oldest brother, Michael. But now they ran down my cheeks as I recounted what the doctor had told us.

Though I was the second youngest of eight kids, in many ways through the years I had become the big brother. They had all remained in Queens and the surrounding area, while my successful career had taken me to several different parts of the country before I finally settled in Virginia. But part of me was always still back there with the rest of them, and I tried to help out in any way that I could and be the one that kept us all in touch with one another.

Exposing my vulnerability and weakness to them was uncomfortable. Lying in a hospital bed in front of my siblings, incapacitated, I felt a little helpless for the first time in as long as I could remember.

"Hey, don't worry, Mark, everything's going to be okay," one of them said.

I tried my best to smile bravely, but inside I was still quite anxious.

Relieved that their summons to the hospital appeared to have been a false alarm, my visitors gave me hugs and their best wishes and left Brenda and me alone again. She had arranged for Jenée to move back to our house from where she was living to look after Markus for the time being. Meanwhile, Brenda stayed with me.

The rest of Sunday passed uneventfully. Brenda stayed with me right through the night as I slept off and on. I didn't feel very relaxed in the hospital, but at least there was no more pain.

On Monday morning I felt fairly normal. One of the doctors came by and asked how I was doing.

"Pretty good, thanks."

"Good. Do you think you can get up and walk? Let's see how you manage."

A little cautiously, I sat up, maneuvered sideways, and put my feet down on the ground. Then I stood up slowly. I felt fine. No dizziness, no head pain, and I could feel my left leg and arm again. I seemed to be back to normal.

The doctor had me walk out of my room and down the hall, telling me to stand close to the wall where there was a railing, in case I needed it. I didn't: I walked down to the end of the hall unaided, turned, and came back.

When I was back in bed, the doctor checked his notes. "I think you're going to be fine, Mr. Moore," he said. "We want to keep you here for a few days, just for observation, but I think by Friday we'll be able to release you and you can go home."

I breathed a sigh of relief—too soon.

CHAPTER 2

"THINGS ARE TOUCH AND GO"

I woke at about three a.m. and remembered that I was in the hospital. Something was different, though. Without looking around, I could tell I was not in the same room where my family had gathered at the foot of my bed. I could feel that my head was wrapped heavily, and I was hooked up to all kinds of tubes. There were a couple running from my arms, and a catheter below the sheets. One line snaked out of my nose while another was somehow attached to my stomach.

Clearly something had happened since yesterday. I lay still, trying to avoid the rising sense of panic. *What's going on here?* I wondered. Looking around, I could see cards and flowers on the cabinet next to me. No, this definitely was not the room in which the doctor had seen Brenda and me and told us I'd be going home in a few days.

I could hear the quiet hum of the bedside equipment I seemed to be plugged into, a range of monitors and machines.

And there was the sound of the television playing quietly in the background, from where it hung on the wall across the room.

Lying still, trying to take everything in, I focused on the broadcast. It was some kind of news program. As one report ended, a male presenter came on to make the link to the next segment. He said something about Father's Day coming this weekend.

Say what? That jarred me further awake. Father's Day? But that was impossible. It was Mother's Day just a couple of days ago...Yet, the man was talking about Father's Day. That was in mid-June: had I just lost a month of my life somewhere? How could more than four weeks have gone by without my knowing about it?

I was too scared to move, even if I had been able to. As I lay there, fragments of memory began to rise. Vague images of people coming into my room. Brenda, of course. Jenée. Mike Wheeler, my business partner and dear friend, and his wife, Teresa. Her father, Dick Lynch.

Unable to put all the pieces together in a picture that made sense, I tried to remain calm and wait quietly. The nurse who came in to check on me sometime later was surprised to find me with my eyes open.

"Oh, Mr. Moore, you're awake," she said brightly.

I acknowledged her with a look, but I didn't try to speak. There were too many scary questions rattling around inside my head. I decided I would just wait until Brenda came. She would have the answers. So I lay quietly, trying not to let my thoughts run away with themselves.

Brenda arrived around nine a.m., a big smile on her face as she walked into the room.

"Tony!" she cried. Brenda had called me by the shortened

version of my middle name, Anthony, from soon after we had first met. She'd decided to do so because she wanted a private, pet name for me, and also to honor an older God-brother and Vietnam vet of whom she was very fond. When she addressed me that way, I knew she was lovingly telling me I was hers in a way no one else was—or, on occasion, that I was in trouble and better listen good. This time, it was full of relief.

She came over and kissed me on my cheek. It was good to feel her touch, a tangible sign that something in my life was still the way it had been.

"You're awake," she said, squeezing my hand. "How are you feeling?"

I mumbled that I was fine, though it was uncomfortable to speak. My throat was sore from the breathing tube that had been inserted for a month.

"What happened, Bren?" I managed to croak.

She patted my arm. "It's so good to see you, Tony, but you shouldn't be talking."

"Okay," I said. "But what happened, Brenda?"

She must have sensed that, as usual, I wasn't going to let something go when I wanted to know. I wouldn't take no for an answer—or no answer.

"What do you remember?" she asked.

Haltingly, I told her about the doctor saying I'd had a mini-stroke but I could go home in a few days, at the end of the week. And now this newscaster had just said that Father's Day was coming soon.

"There's a long time between Mother's Day and Father's Day," I said. "Something must have happened to me. What?"

Recognizing that I wasn't going to let go of this, and maybe to keep me from talking more, Brenda took a deep breath.

"Well, it turns out that you didn't have a mini-stroke," she said. "It was a full-blown one."

As I took that in, she went on, "And then you actually had a second stroke on the Monday after. They had to do emergency surgery, but you're all right now."

I let that sink in for a moment.

"Wow, okay. So when am I coming home?"

"You're not," she said. "We're going to transfer to another hospital."

I was confused. I'd had surgery and things were fine, so why wasn't I being discharged? I sensed that Brenda wasn't telling me the whole story.

"You had two strokes," she said. "It's pretty serious and you have a long recovery ahead of you." She tried to smile to be encouraging. "You're going to be fine, but we need to work on your recovery. They want you to go to another hospital that can help with that."

I could tell that she was a bit uncomfortable, not really wanting to be telling me all this so soon after I had woken, so I didn't push her for any more details. I was quite shocked by what she had said, but at the same time I was glad to know. I'd always wanted to face things head-on and deal with them, rather than tiptoe around them. The information might be tough to deal with, I figured, but at least once it was out there, it was a known quantity and I didn't have to worry about something worse being revealed.

Brenda stayed with me through the rest of the day. She told me a little more about what had happened in the days and weeks that had passed without my knowing. Apparently I'd gradually been brought out of my induced coma the previous day, when doctors removed the breathing tube from my throat. I'd blinked once for yes and twice for no in answer to a series of questions gauging my physical status—what parts of my body I could feel and move—and my memory and comprehension: did I know who I was, and who Brenda was? I'd been told not to try to speak with the breathing tube still in place; it would be removed later that day. I'd been handed a pad of paper on which to write questions and answers, too, but I had no recollection of any of this.

It was a lot to take in. Much of the day I spent quietly with my thoughts, my grogginess receding as the anesthetic level in my body dropped. I was so glad to have Brenda's caring, comforting presence as I tried to piece things together in my mind.

I had missed plenty during those lost four weeks, I would learn later: moments of anguish, long hours of alarm, and days of anxiety for Brenda and my friends and loved ones.

Though the doctor's TIA/mini-stroke verdict on the Sunday and my ability to walk without problems the following day had reduced her level of concern, Brenda had opted to stay in the hospital with me for that third night.

Her decision may have saved my life.

The headache came back sometime later on Monday. Nowhere near the pain level that had left me curled in a ball two days earlier, but uncomfortable enough for me to need some relief. I was given more painkiller, which made me a bit woozy, leaving me drifting in and out of sleep.

I woke around three a.m. and Brenda was there, watching over me. We talked about being discharged later in the week and how the kids were coping at home without us. I started to get a little agitated about something and then suddenly just cut out in the middle of the conversation, like someone had flipped a switch. Darkness.

Perturbed, Brenda leaned over me in the bed to take a closer look. Pulling the sheets back, she noticed that one of my legs was quite badly swollen. She brought this to the attention of one of the nurses, who seemed unconcerned. I'd been getting lots of IV fluids, the nurse said, and being immobile might have caused a bit of buildup; that was all. Nothing to worry about.

Brenda doesn't usually flash her medical credentials in front of other health professionals when family is involved; she prefers to be mom or wife, as required. But something about my condition that night did not sit right with her.

She politely explained to the nurse that she had some medical training, then set out her reasons for her concern. "I really think we need to reach out to the doctor who is responsible for him," she said.

When Brenda was told that the neurologist wouldn't be available until later in the morning, she decided enough was enough. "I don't think we ought to wait that long," she said, explaining all her concerns: my sudden incoherence and agitation, the swelling, the lack of clarity about the cause of my apparent TIA.

Her insistence finally prevailed, and I was taken for a scan at about six a.m. Brenda's intervention was crucial, she would learn. Nurses came a little while later and told her that a doctor arriving on duty had passed near where my scans were on display and glanced over. What she saw alarmed her, and she paused to take a closer look, they said, announcing that whoever this patient was needed lifesaving surgery—right away. She was canceling her planned patient list and was going to prep to operate on me immediately, they said.

Sometime later a doctor came to the family waiting area where Brenda had by now been joined by Rochelle, who was staying at our house with Jenée and Markus, and the Wheelers. Other family members were on their way to the hospital.

Dr. Anje Kim introduced herself as a neurosurgeon on staff at the hospital, though I was not one of her patients. "I've looked at your husband's CAT scan, and I am concerned," she told Brenda.

"There's a lot of pressure building up in his brain, too much pressure. I don't know what's causing that, but things are touch and go. We need to do surgery urgently to try to relieve some of that pressure, and insert a shunt to drain away any fluid or blood. I'm going to clear my schedule to do this right away. I don't know exactly what we are going to find when we get in there, but I promise you I will do my best. I need you to sign these consent forms right away."

Though she was direct with Brenda, Dr. Kim did not reveal the full measure of her concern. But what she had seen on my scans had prompted her to call for immediate major brain surgery, the kind that was usually transferred to another hospital in the area with a more advanced line of services. There was no time to lose.

What had been downplayed as a TIA was actually a major and somewhat rare hemorrhagic stroke—the kind that occurs in around only one in eight cases. Most strokes are ischemic, when blood flow to the brain is blocked, often by a blood clot. They typically affect older people and are often associated with aging, hypertension, heart problems, or other chronic illness. I'd suffered a vertebral artery dissection, which usually occurs in people slightly younger than I was and can often result from some kind of injury, such as whiplash in a car accident, though I'd not hurt myself recently.

Whatever the cause, one of the arteries in the back of my

neck had started getting blocked. Eventually the pressure built up so much that the artery burst, spilling blood into my brain and causing it to swell—hence the headaches.

The swelling was preventing the normal flow of cerebrospinal fluid, which bathes the brain and acts as a buffer against shock, sort of like a car's suspension. As my brain began to swell, it caused this fluid to back up, further adding to the pressure from the pooling blood. This was all happening close to my brain stem, the cerebellum. The part of the brain that is responsible for motor function, it had to be protected at all costs; if that were to be impaired, I would lose all mental and physical capacity. When a person's brain stem is damaged severely, he or she is considered to be brain dead.

Acting quickly, Dr. Kim led a team that opened up the back of my skull, creating a hole through which my squeezed brain could expand, critically releasing the built-up pressure. Having also opened the membrane that encased my brain, to help relieve the internal pressure, Dr. Kim then covered the exposed brain tissue with a protective collagen barrier, somewhat like a sterile gel patch.

After two hours in the OR, Dr. Kim had done all that she could. "I think we have been able to save his life," she told Brenda. "But his condition is grave. At this stage we do not know what the long-term effects of the swelling will be. We'll be watching him very carefully for the next twenty-four to forty-eight hours to see what happens."

She explained that I would be held in a medically induced coma for some time, to ensure that I was kept as immobilized as possible. The smallest movement could be unhelpful as my brain recovered and the swelling went down. Not only would I be kept unconscious; my head would be secured in position to make sure there was no potentially jarring movement.

Dr. Kim explained things as simply as she could, unaware that Brenda's nursing training meant she knew exactly what was going on. Nor did Dr. Kim realize that Brenda was carefully evaluating everything she was saying. So when she used the word *grave* to describe my condition, Brenda knew my situation was still really serious: doctors and nurses would typically avoid such strong language whenever possible.

With Rochelle and the Wheelers close by, Brenda slumped to the ground and screamed. "No! He can't leave now. He has too much to do. It's not time."

But she didn't stay down for long. Brenda quickly rose to become a tower of strength for all the family over the next four-plus weeks.

Equally relieved to see each other again, Brenda and I spent much of the rest of the day quietly after I woke up. Speaking was uncomfortable because my throat was still sore from having the breathing tube removed, but we'd talk a little as I asked her how the children were doing, about the family, and what had been happening at work. But I could tell that she didn't want me to strain myself or to tax me with too much information right away, and it was good just to lie there silently between doctors' visits and nurses' checks and know we were together.

And I was still trying to take in all the facts: two strokes, four weeks of oblivion, the full extent of the damage was unknown, and it was unclear how much longer I would be in the hospital.

Then, around six p.m., Brenda sat forward. "I'm going to go home now, Tony."

I was surprised, a little hurt. I'd been unconscious for most of a month; I was confused and scared about what lay ahead. She'd told me she had stayed in the room with me every night since the strokes, and now that I was awake she was going to leave me on my own? It didn't make any sense.

"You must be tired," she said. "You need to get some rest. I'm going to go home and check on Jenée and Markus."

After she left, disappointment at Brenda's departure gave way to anger at God. *Why did He let this happen to me? I'm a pretty good person. This just isn't fair.* Resentment bubbled away inside as I lay unable to move.

Brenda had been right as she left: I was tired. Though I had spent much of the last four weeks asleep, I woke up feeling exhausted. Even just thinking was tiring. But now that I was alone, my mind continued to whir. I tried to think through what I was facing, attempting to evaluate everything methodically, as I would a business situation. The prospects scared me, and anger began to give way to defeat and hopelessness.

Maybe I'll never get out of this bed, I thought. Unable to find the drive that usually powered me through challenges, not really even wanting to try, I resigned myself to being handicapped. Things needn't be so bad, I tried to rationalize. I had money that could make life much easier for me. I'd adapt and survive. I was still alive, after all.

The flood of emotions I had experienced in the few hours I had been awake, combined with the medications I was being given, made me groggy. I would doze for a while, come to, and then slip away again.

At one awakening, somewhere during the night, this was in my mind: *God only gives you what He knows you can handle.*

The words came out of nowhere and from a long time ago,

but I knew immediately from whose lips: Mom's. It was some-thing she had told me and my brothers and sisters time and again in our busy home in Queens. It was offered as an encour-agement, a promise, a comfort, and a challenge to get up and keep going. *God only gives you what He knows you can handle.*

Curious: I hadn't thought about that exhortation of hers in more than thirty years. I had accepted it as good motherly wis-dom at the time, but somewhere in the intervening years it had been put on a back shelf—along with any serious consideration of faith.

I believed in God in a vague way. Both Brenda and I had been raised in churchgoing homes, a commitment we had con-tinued throughout our life together. I considered myself a good person; I loved my wife, I provided for my family, I cared for my friends, I treated my employees and business associates well, and I always said please and thank you.

But I essentially approached faith this way: I'd give God a couple of hours on Sunday morning but then take charge for the rest of the week. I had been pretty sure that He was okay with that, for much of my life, although my brush with death had left me wondering whether I was maybe being punished for something.

Now, unexpectedly, *God only gives you what He knows you can handle.* I turned it over in my head and drifted off to sleep again.

Another old memory popped to mind when I next awoke: John Wooden, the legendary "Wizard of Westwood" basketball coach at UCLA. As a big basketball fan, I'd long admired him for his achievements—six-time national coach of the year—and the principled character he had displayed.

I recalled reading his book *Wooden: A Lifetime of Observa-tions and Reflections On and Off the Court* while we were living in

Greenville, South Carolina, back in the late nineties. I'd been interested in the sports stuff but more intrigued by his lessons on leadership, as I was keen to learn all I could as my business opportunities and responsibilities grew.

Now, in the hospital, I remembered how Wooden had written about what he said were the three most important foundations of a man's life—his faith, his family, and his friends. I wondered why that had come to mind after so long, and then I drifted away once more.

When I woke the next time, something had shifted. It was as though different pieces of a puzzle had fallen into place while I slept. I found myself offering a mental prayer.

God, please just give me the strength for whatever You send my way.

I didn't feel resentful anymore. I didn't ask Him to let me walk again. I didn't try to negotiate: "If You do this, then I will do that." I just let go. For the first time in my life, I simply surrendered. It was a foreign experience, but it felt good. Peaceful.

If I could have gotten myself out of bed, I would have sunk to my knees. Instead, I just lay there, my stillness a symbol that I wasn't going to try to make anything happen.

I knew that I faced a big challenge. But I was confident that with His help—and yes, with the support of my friends and family—I could deal with whatever was ahead.

God, please just give me the strength for whatever You send my way.

CHAPTER 3

"FOCUS ON WHAT
YOU NEED"

I never served in the military, but growing up in a family of ten in Jamaica, Queens, was a bit like an extended boot camp. Our two-bedroom home on 171st Street was where I learned about duty, discipline, diligence, and devotion.

Our parents viewed their small, eight-hundred-square-foot wooden house as a sort of Fort Moore, an outpost in hostile territory. The chain-link fence that ran around the property both kept the wider world out and kept us in. Their concern was well earned; the area was one of the toughest neighborhoods in New York City's largest borough. It was not uncommon to hear gunshots, and one time our mailbox was riddled with bullet holes.

When I was old enough to be allowed out and about on my own, I quickly learned which routes to avoid, so as not to walk into potential danger areas. I don't remember seeing any police officers around, ordinarily; they seemed to venture into the neighborhood only when necessary.

With ten people under one small roof, home ran rather like

a barracks. The four girls—Sharon, Joanne, Rochelle, Donna—doubled up in two beds in one room, while I and my three brothers—Michael, Greg, Gary—did the same in the other. Mom and Dad were left to sleep in the family room, pulling down a sofa bed at night when the rest of us were asleep. They kept their clothes in the basement, which they eventually converted into a room of their own.

With just one bathroom, there was a strict order of use in the mornings. Mom, the family quartermaster in her housecoat uniform, created a schedule based on what time we had to be out of the house for the particular school we were attending. Heaven forbid you were not ready for your turn!

Dad was the drill sergeant. A firm disciplinarian, he believed that if one of us boys stepped out of line, we would never really learn our lesson without the benefit of a good whupping. Typically he would use his belt, but serious infractions would send him out into the backyard to pull a good switch from one of the trees.

Usually we did something wrong to earn a punishment, even if what he meted out would be considered excessive by today's standards. But sometimes it felt like he could be straight-out unfair, as far as we were concerned.

When I was about seven years old, we got Caesar, a German shepherd. The first day we had him, we were playing out in the yard excitedly when he ran into the bench next to the picnic table. Caesar's yelp brought Dad out fuming.

"Have you broken that animal's leg?" he demanded.

No, we told him, we hadn't touched Caesar; he just bumped into the bench on his own. But we each got a spanking all the same.

In middle school, my class basketball team made it to the semifinal of the annual championship. After-school tip-off at three thirty p.m. meant that I could play and just make it home ahead of our five p.m. curfew.

It turned out to be a close game, going to overtime, in which I made the winning shot. Elated, I ran all the way home, but it was five minutes after the hour when I got in the door.

Dad looked up from where he was sitting in the kitchen. "What time is it, son?"

Still pumped by our achievement, I told him about the game running late and my victory shot.

"Yeah," he said. "But five-oh-five isn't five. You're benched."

Crestfallen, I told him the final was to be played the next day. I begged him to let me play.

"Nope. You're not playing, and that's that."

There was no debating Dad once he had made his mind up. The next day, when my classmates asked me if I was ready for the big game after school, I said sure, not wanting to admit what had happened. When school finished I said I needed to go home for something, but I'd be back. Instead I sat in my room and stewed.

The following day I made some excuse for not turning up to play, pretending I had fallen sick.

As well as learning to follow the rules to the letter, we were also taught about hard work. A house of ten meant there were always plenty of dishes to be cleaned and dried by hand—we couldn't afford a dishwasher—and then there was yard work and trips to the grocery.

Dad may have barked the most orders, but we all knew that, behind the scenes, Mom was really commander in chief. For instance, Dad liked to go out for a drink and a smoke with his friends and to gamble a little, but that wasn't allowed in the house, and he followed directions.

They made a good team and were committed to each other and their kids, and though they didn't display many outward signs of affection, we always knew that we were loved. Above all, they emphasized the importance of us being family, and how we always needed to have one another's backs. We were paired off with a "battle buddy" closest to our age.

That left me keeping an eye out for Gary, just over a year younger than me. He was a bit of a wild kid who liked to stir things up, which led to his getting into a fight when he and I were over at the park one day. I kept an eye on him but didn't intervene, and he came out of the scuffle the loser.

When we got home, Mom asked me if I had tried to help break things up. When I told her no, it was one of the few times she ever got angry with me.

"That's your brother," she said firmly. "Family. If he needs help, you help."

I remembered that subsequently when Gary brawled with another kid at the park. His opponent took a licking and ran off, only to return a short while later with his older brother, who was wielding a knife and insisting on a rematch.

Stilled by the blade at first, I stood and watched the two boys fight again until a ring on his opponent's hand left Gary with a swollen eye. Mom's directive came back to me.

"Okay, enough," I said, stepping between the two younger boys and the kid with the knife. "We're done," I said, trying to come off as assertive. "That's it." Thankfully I must have sounded convincing enough for the older boy with the knife to back down, and Gary and I managed to walk away without further harm.

On another occasion I had to fight an older boy at school when he started picking on Donna: I knew what Mom needed me to do. And as I got older and a bit bigger, I was expected to meet my sisters at work when they had finished and walk them home if it was dark.

I wasn't as ready to mix things up as Gary, who could be pretty volatile. But I did learn to take care of myself. That was just part and parcel of growing up in Jamaica, Queens. Other kids would test you, and you had to let them know that you weren't going to be pushed around. If I could talk my way out of something without losing face, I would. And I would be judicious about who I would take on; no point picking bigger opponents if you didn't have to.

But there were occasions when there was no choice. One day in middle school, a kid came up to me in the cafeteria and told me to move because I was in his seat. He wasn't interested in my reasonably pointing out that I'd been sitting there for ages, and with so many eyes on us I couldn't just walk away. That would be a sign of weakness.

The principal had to be summoned to break us up, and he called our parents to report the fracas. Given Dad's insistence on our respect for authority and doing well at school, I was apprehensive when I got home later that day. He was waiting for me at the front door.

"The principal called and told me you were fighting, son."

I nodded.

"Did you start it?"

I shook my head. "No, Dad. The other kid did."

"You did good," he told me. "You don't go starting a fight, but you need to stand up for yourself if one comes to you. I'm proud of you."

That unexpected exchange revealed some of the tenderness behind his toughness. For all his unyielding ways, Dad's discipline and strictness ultimately came from a place of love. So while I feared his wrath if I stepped out of line, at the same time I was never simply scared of him.

And, on occasion, his dry humor would shine through. He loved to play games with us, like Uno, when he'd cheat with a twinkle in his eye, maybe putting down a six in place of a nine and hoping we wouldn't notice.

If he was winning, he'd laugh, saying, "Are you scared? If so, you can jump in my pocket right now!"

Dad's strict ways came not just from having one eye on his own past, which included six years in the army, but from training the other on our futures, believing we must be protected from bad influences if we were to get ahead. He saw his heavy oversight as a way he could help his children, providing structure and security even if he could not provide many material things.

This was behind his refusal to let us out of the yard to play unsupervised when we were young. It was just too dangerous for us to be out in the neighborhood on our own, he and Mom would tell us. All the other kids would pass by on their way to nearby Liberty Park, which we could see across and just down the street, and taunt us as we watched from behind the fence. "Are you in a zoo or something?"

They would make fun of us, yelling that it was crazy that we were stuck behind a barrier, like we were in prison. To the contrary, we thought the craziness was out there.

By the time I reached about fifth grade, I was allowed to go down to Liberty Park, but I still had to be home before the sun went down; there was to be absolutely no hanging out there after dark.

My parents' caution was well-founded. Though neither was as widespread as they would become in the years that followed, drugs and gangs were simply a part of everyday life. By the time I was in middle school, most of the kids I knew in the neighborhood were experimenting with weed and booze—typically snuck from their parents' supplies.

I was never tempted to dabble, initially because Dad had made it absolutely clear that there would be serious consequences if we were ever caught messing around like that. He told us that if ever we got into any trouble, there would be a "discussion." Fear can be a strong motivator for making right choices.

At that stage in my life, it was definitely more of a driver than faith. My parents were religious, but in a slightly detached kind of way. For them, religion was more about what we did, how we behaved, than what we might have really believed deep inside. There was just a right way to live, they maintained.

For Dad, that sometimes meant do what he said, not what he did: take his smoking and drinking. He didn't go to church, but Mom took us when we were young and insisted we continue to attend on our own when we got older. As she had been raised Roman Catholic, we would troop off to St. Benedict the Moor Church on 110th Avenue each Sunday. I completed catechism classes—a seemingly endless round of boring Saturday mornings is all I recall—along with Sharon, Joanne, Rochelle, Donna, and Gary, and took my First Communion.

We'd say a brief grace at home before meals, and we were encouraged to say our bedtime prayers, but that was about the extent of our spiritual life together. I accepted that there was a God, but as far as I could tell He was a rather remote figure, looking down on us from on high, checking that we were follow-ing His rules—with Dad serving as his lieutenant.

But if avoiding Dad's displeasure rather than pleasing God was my main reason for keeping out of trouble, I discovered another motivation as I got older: this one positive rather than negative. Doing the right thing didn't only save me from punishment, I found out; it also brought its own rewards.For as long as I could remember, our parents had wanted more for us than they had known themselves. That desire to get ahead had brought them to New York City in the first place. Like many African Ameri-cans living in the South in the mid-twentieth century, they had looked north for a better life.

James Moore was born in Greensboro, North Carolina, on February 10, 1930. Lollie Ruger came into the world across the state line, in Yemassee, South Carolina, on March 13, 1931. They met when they arrived in New York as young adults, hoping to improve their prospects.

Married on October 12, 1951, they had soon started a fam-ily, Dad working a variety of physical labor jobs until he landed a secure position with the New York City Transit Authority. Their first home was a rented apartment near Lincoln Street, in the Baisley Park area of Queens.

By the time I arrived on March 25, 1961, space was at a premium. Gary's arrival the following year only added to the squeeze. With all of us, the home my parents managed to save for on 171st Street was still small, but it was theirs.

Glad as they were to have made the progress they did, they hoped we might go further. Doing so would require diligence, they emphasized. And coasting was not an option: when high school graduation came, it was college, a job, or the military. There would be no just hanging around at home, living off them. Within weeks of graduation, both my older brothers, Michael and Greg, went off to the navy.

Michael and a couple of my sisters took a few college classes before choosing other options, deciding that further school was not for them. Neither of my parents had gone to college either, so when I began to show an aptitude in the classroom at an early age, it initially caught them by surprise.

My first teachers all encouraged my efforts, warming me toward education. I found myself coming first on a lot of the tests, my name often being called out in front of the other kids for doing so well. I liked the feeling, though I was careful not to brag about my successes: Mom didn't stand for any showboating. I was a big fan of boxer Muhammad Ali, a hero to many African Americans for his ability, charisma, and confidence, but she had no time for the way he preened and badmouthed his opponents.

Naturally, not all the other kids liked the way I would get singled out for attention. Wearing thick, black-framed spectacles from around the second grade to correct my nearsightedness, I earned the nicknames "Peabody" and "Poindexter," after the two brainy cartoon characters that sported similar glasses.

If those early years in school kindled a love of learning, it was Mrs. Wright, my fifth-grade teacher at P.S. 116 elementary school, who lit a fire under me. "You're special, Mark," she would tell me. "You have talent; you can really be something if you want to." Hearing those words of affirmation made me want to try harder, so that she might speak them again.

Mrs. Wright might have been my first childhood crush, not

just because of her encouragement but also because she reminded me a bit of actress Diahann Carroll, the star of the hit television series *Julia*. Not only was she a good educator; she was a good reader of people. One time she was supervising our class as we played a game of punchball out in the schoolyard. My team was getting pounded so badly that I gave up. I walked off, going over to the fence to sit down and sulk. The other kids complained to Mrs. Wright about my desertion, but she ignored me and told them just to keep on playing without me.

Things went from bad to worse for my team as I sat there, and eventually my frustration turned to resolve. I jumped up, went back into the game, and channeled my irritation. Someone needed to take charge, so I did, calling out orders to the rest of the team. Somehow, we managed to claw our way back into the game and eventually won.

As we headed back inside at the end of recess, Mrs. Wright came up beside me. "You're probably wondering why I didn't say anything," she said. Actually, I was thinking more about my mixed feelings—pride that we had come from behind to win, some embarrassment about my initial reaction, stomping off like that.

"I wanted you to figure things out by yourself," Mrs. Wright told me. "You did well, Mark. You quit, and then on your own you decided to come back in. I am impressed. You're a leader, you know."

My parents learned of my progress at school through report cards and teacher conferences. They were encouraging without wanting to make too much of a fuss about it, cautious about singling me out over my siblings. "Mark's just different; that's all," they would say. All they required was that each of us did our best according to our own abilities, though there were times when my brothers and sisters got fed up with hearing about my latest good grades.

Dad had always emphasized that, as African Americans, we would need to hustle and work harder if we wanted to get ahead, to get out of where we were living. "Life isn't fair," he told us flatly.

As I did well at school, earning encouragement from teachers and my parents, I began to think that maybe I had what it would take to find a life beyond Jamaica, Queens. That positive lure became another reason for me to avoid the temptations many of my school friends were beginning to fall into.

There were incidents that further fueled my desire to do well, to secure my ticket out of there. For my seventh-grade science project I needed some mice from a pet store on Jamaica Avenue, a few minutes' walk from the house. My parents gave me the money, and I headed off there one Sunday afternoon with my cousin Ronald, who was in the same class at school. We stopped on the way at a small café to buy a slice of pizza and a soda with the spare change, a rare treat.

As we left, two men confronted us on the street.

"Hey, have you got any money?"

"No," I answered. The next thing I knew, I was on the ground, having been coldcocked. Scared, I got up, and Ronald and I ran off down the street with the two men in pursuit. We hid among the shelves at the back of the pet store, and when the two guys came in after us I found the proprietor and whispered to him to please call the police. He didn't want anything to do with that, simply demanding that the two men leave. Ronald and I waited a while before buying the mice I needed, then ran all the way home with our hearts pumping wildly.

Nor was that the only occasion on which I found myself in the middle of a scary confrontation. Another time my sister

Rochelle and I had been sent down to a local store to buy one of Dad's beloved candy bars for him. We were hunting out one of his favorites on the shelves when we heard a commotion up at the cash register.

"Everyone, get down, he's got a gun!" someone shouted.

Rochelle and I dropped to the floor. There was a gunshot, and the sound of someone slamming out through the door. I think whoever had tried to rob the store had shot into the air, but we did not hang around to find out. Rochelle and I lit out of there and ran for home, without Dad's candy.

These kinds of experiences taught me about always being on the alert, about the need to be tuned in to what was going on around me and to be aware of potential dangers. They helped me develop an ability to gauge situations and get a sense of people's moods and attitudes. They added street smarts to the skills I was developing at school, and they motivated me to work hard so that maybe one day I wouldn't have to live in a place where I had to keep looking over my shoulder every time I went out.

I didn't know I had been poor as a kid until I became rich as an adult. When I began to have enough money to do some of the things I wanted—not just needed—to do, I realized how little we had gotten by with back in Queens. Not surprising, given that Mom and Dad were raising a family of ten on his income from the transit authority. But they never let on how difficult it must have been for them to manage, nor complained about having to go without themselves so we could have the essentials.

The closest Dad ever got to talking about our standard of living was the advice he began giving when I got into high school. "Son, focus on what you need, not what you want," he would tell me. "We want a lot of things in life, but we need very little. Just try to focus on what you need." The cupboards in our house were never empty, but there wasn't a lot of choice. Mom always made sure that we had the basics, like bread and milk. We ate a lot of chicken—cooked just about every way you can imagine—and rice in the winter. Summertime there would be cold cuts. We didn't have cookies and soda, nor did we ever get to eat fast food; Mom could cater for us more cheaply at home. Going to the movies wasn't part of our family lifestyle either; we made do with the one black-and-white television in the family room.

There wasn't much spare money for celebrations. We'd usually get a card on our birthday, but that was it. There would be a gift at Christmas—one each. My wardrobe also consisted of a lot of second- and third-hand pass-ons, which could be a bit difficult given that Michael and Greg were quite a few years older than me and of course that much bigger. I had to use rubber bands to hold up the athletic socks I inherited.

One thing I was glad to receive from them was their discarded comic books. A keen reader, I devoured Marvel and DC Comics superhero adventures: Spider-Man, the Incredible Hulk, the Fantastic Four. Something about them inspired me, the way they seemed like ordinary people until they tapped into that secret side of them that set them apart from everyone else. I was drawn to how they always tried to make the world a better place for others.

I'd spend hours reading in my room, where I also consumed Matt Christopher's adventure books for kids. I loved how most of the plots unfolded in the sporting world. When I wasn't reading about sports I'd be watching them on the television or practicing outside. Sitting down to watch together when games were being broadcast was one way I got to spend time with Dad. Unlike most New Yorkers, he'd follow both the Yankees and the Mets, an unusual shared loyalty I would continue. I would also watch the Knicks and was one of the few African American kids in the area I knew who liked ice hockey, cheering on the Rangers.

Though I loved to play sports, I didn't get to do so as part of a team much. For starters, I wasn't allowed outside the yard when I was young. Then when I was of an age where I could venture a bit farther afield, we didn't have the money to join any organized programs.

So I would spend hours practicing on my own. I'd rehearse free throws, layups, and rebounds on the basketball hoop we had in the backyard. I'd use a broom handle to perfect my baseball swing, tossing a stone up into the air to aim at. The narrowness of my "bat" gave me a pretty good eye.

One day I was out on my imaginary diamond when I pulled my swing and fired the rock off to my left. Crash! The window in the house next door shattered.

Panicked, I quickly hid the broom handle and ran inside before anyone could see me. I thought I was in the clear until a few days later, when Dad said to me casually, "By the way, son, the neighbors told me you broke their window."

Uh-oh. Now I was in trouble. I stammered an explanation. "I thought I was hitting them good, but I pulled one," I said. "I'm sorry."

There was a pause, then: "Don't worry. I paid them for it. Just don't do it again."

I breathed a sigh of relief. No spanking. This wasn't like the Dad I knew when I was younger, but as I got a bit older his tough stance would waver occasionally. Maybe he was just getting tired; I was the seventh of eight children, so he'd been at the parenting thing hard and long for a good while by the time I was beginning to grow older.

Once I was allowed beyond the fence, I'd play in the streets, where parked cars marked the limits of our football "field," or over at Liberty Park. Many times I would team up with my best friend, Lenny Richards. He lived in the neighborhood and came from a similarly protective home, so we had a lot in common. Though we went to different schools—his parents could afford for him to attend the Catholic one—we hung out together as much as possible.

Another reason I didn't consider myself to be poor when I was a kid, beyond my parents' refusal to focus on what they didn't have, was that most of the other people I knew didn't have much either, so there was nothing to contrast our basic lifestyle with.

One exception was Don, an older cousin. He and his family lived out on Long Island, and we would see them on big holidays like Memorial Day and July Fourth. Don was a banker who wore a suit and tie to work and carried a briefcase. He was the only African American I knew who dressed like that. I thought it must be pretty cool to leave the house like that each morning. Aspiring to be like him one day was another impetus for me to apply myself at school.

There was a moment when our lack of money looked like it could impede my education efforts, however. When I reached middle school, I was selected to be part of a group of thirty or so students who were singled out for our academic abilities. We were told that if we maintained strong grades all the way through, when it came time to go on to high school we could pass over a whole school year and start as tenth graders rather than ninth graders.

I'd forgotten all about that by the time middle school came to an end, but it turned out that I was one of only two students still eligible to leapfrog our incoming high school year. Not only that, but I'd done well enough to be considered for a place at Brooklyn Tech, with its specialization in engineering, math, and science.

This was a pretty prestigious opportunity, and my junior high teachers encouraged my parents to let me go there, saying it would be a great way to stretch me. But Mom and Dad were still cautious and protective, even as they had loosened up a little. They were not keen on the idea of me traveling into the city on my own, as I would need to.

So Jamaica High School it would be, only there was one problem. The city had recently introduced a policy that required all incoming students to provide medical and dental records. Now age fourteen, I had never been to the dentist in my life, not even for a checkup. When it came to health issues in our family, the approach was: if you are not sick, we don't need to go spending limited money on unnecessary appointments.

Dad wasn't happy when I told him about it. "You got a problem? You got a toothache?"

"No, Dad," I said, "but they say I have to have dental records to go to high school."

He seemed to grumble to himself for a moment, then: "Well, then, I guess you've got to go to the dentist." Somehow they found the money.

It wasn't only money that was at a premium in our home, however. So was space; with ten of us under one small roof, there was always someone else around. Living in such close quarters taught me two things that would prove advantageous later in life: focus and forgiveness. I developed an ability to tune out distractions so I could concentrate on what I needed to do.

I also learned to let go of things that didn't really matter, not to hold on to petty grievances. With so many of us in close proximity, there could almost always be something to bug me, if I let it.

CHAPTER 4

"FIND SOMEONE WHO IS NICE AND SMART"

At Jamaica High School I discovered the two things that would forever change my life. I found I had a rare gift for numbers, and I found my number one.

The transition from Richard S. Grossley Middle School, or I.S. 8 as it was also known, was a bit of a stretch. I was jumping over a grade, starting my high school life among tenth graders, who'd already had a year to adjust to the ways things were in this new teenage environment. For someone who came from a fairly sheltered harbor, I was now in rather open seas.

I didn't tell anyone that I had skipped a grade; there didn't seem to be any good reason to set myself apart. Letting others know I was a year younger might single me out for unwelcome special attention. So I just let everyone assume that I had recently moved to the area or maybe transferred from another school.

Jamaica High was only about a mile from home, but it extended the territory of my world and broadened my horizons.

Where the student body at I.S. 8 had been one hundred percent African American, I was now in the minority. Drawing from other, more mixed neighborhoods in the catchment area, the rest of the student population, much larger than my junior high, were white, Asian, Hispanic, and Middle Eastern.

I enjoyed almost all my classes. Social studies and history intrigued me—I loved to read about the Civil War and the two world wars and to try to understand why people and groups of people made the decisions they did. But I came even more alive with math. Having taken an accelerated program while at I.S. 8, I'd already studied—and aced—algebra, geometry, and calculus.

I liked the order and predictability of numbers: if you handled them correctly, there was always a right answer. And it wasn't just something down on paper; it translated into real life. I combined my flair for numbers with my love of sports, studying baseball players' batting averages and football players' rushing yards. I'd look for the latest stats in the newspaper each day the same way I'd later check my stocks.

Given both my decision to keep my head down to avoid questions about my academic bent and my natural shyness, I didn't go out of my way to make new friends. But I did spot someone among the crowd of kids I'd pass through in the halls who made me turn my head. A curly Afro crowned her cute face, set with bright eyes. She dressed more conservatively than many of the other girls—button-up tops and modest skirts, no trousers allowed—who looked like they were getting ready to go out to a nightclub, and she carried herself with a quietly confident poise.

I was smitten from a distance, but I'd never have thought of trying to speak to her. Even if I'd had the confidence, Mom and

Dad had made it quite clear that they thought I was too young to be getting involved with girls and that I needed to concentrate on my schooling. So I just noticed her from afar.

And then I found myself sitting next to her.

Band class was a waste of time, as far as I was concerned. But I had to take a music class of some kind and band seemed to be the best of the options, so I reluctantly turned up with the trombone I'd tried to learn for a couple of years in junior high. In our first class we were seated in alphabetical order, which is how I came to be seated by a girl with a trumpet whose name was Brenda Moore.

More outgoing than I, she introduced herself with a smile. I managed to mumble a reply.

This seating arrangement was a pleasant surprise, but our first real interaction did not seem to bode well.

The problem was, I did not take band class seriously. To me it was just a waste of time. I was never going to continue playing, and there were more important things I could be doing with my time. Like homework. And that is what I did.

Sitting toward the back of the room, I'd get my trombone out and put my music sheets on my stand. Then I'd dig out my other classes' books and papers and just do my homework while everyone else played, hidden behind my stand and looking up occasionally to check that the teacher, Mr. Stein, hadn't called on me.

By now, we'd been separated into our respective sections, which left Brenda still close by. She leaned over toward me one day.

"Hey, do you mind if I ask you a question?"

"Sure, what's up?"

"How come you don't play your instrument?" She sounded a little bit put out that I was shirking.

I told her that I didn't like it and preferred to do my homework. She laughed. "Well, okay, but you really should play, you know."

My band deception worked well for the first few weeks of the class. Then, one day, in the middle of a passage, Mr. Stein held his hands up and halted everyone.

"Hold up, hold up a minute," he said. "I just want to hear the trombones."

I knew I was in trouble. Not having played in several months, I'd doubtless lost the strength and tone in my cheeks. That proved to be the case when I lifted the trombone to my lips, pursed, and blew, and nothing came out.

Mr. Stein frowned, confused. "Mark," he said. "I want you to do me a favor: go in the side room there and practice on your own, would you?" I gathered up my things, walked into the rehearsal room, closed the door—and got my homework out again.

If I thought that I had pulled one over on Mr. Stein, I was sadly mistaken. But I found out only when report card time came. There it was in black and white, my interim grade for band class: D. I was horrified; for as long as I could remember I had pulled only As. How was I ever going to explain this to my parents? Surely this was going to lead to a "discussion" with my father, with its painful conclusion.

I decided that the only course of action was straight-up honesty. When Dad queried the terrible grade, I told him, "Well, to be honest, Dad, I really don't like playing the trombone. But I've not been just been goofing off in class—I've been using the time to do my homework." Then I waited.

He was silent for a while, just looking at the report card and then at me. "I tell you what, son," he said. "Here's what's going to happen." I braced myself.

"You're going to stop doing your homework in class, and you're going to start playing your trombone, okay?" I nodded. "Because I don't want to see another D on the next report card."

Relieved to walk away without a scolding, I learned my lesson. Or at least part of it. I did stop doing my homework in band class: I just did it in gym class, instead.

I finished out my band classes playing trombone faithfully if not enthusiastically. The following semester I rotated to gym. While I enjoyed sports, I did not like what we had to do for gym class: forward rolls, trampoline jumps, things like that. It seemed like another huge waste of time. To start with, I'd dress for gym, then slide off up to the bleachers with my book bag and do my homework. After a while, I stopped even bothering to change and just went and sat down to study.

I really should not have been surprised when my interim report card included my second-ever D, this time for gym.

Dad's eyes went wide when he saw it. "Didn't we talk about this last semester?" he demanded.

I was sure there'd be a beating this time. "Yes, Dad," I said. "I'm sorry. I was doing my homework again."

Maybe it was the fact that I'd been working, not just shirking again. Or maybe it was another example of how he was just getting tired of laying down the law after so long. Either way, Dad looked at me.

"Here's what is going to happen," he said. "You're going to get dressed for gym, you're going to jump on that trampoline, and you're going to do your forward rolls and whatever else you are told to do, okay? Because I do not want to see another D. Am I clear? Do you understand me?"

There was a finality to his tone that told me this was his last concession. I decided not to test my judgment.

High school did see some gradual loosening of the ties that bound us to home. When I got into the tenth grade, I got a job at Queens Public Library on Merrick Boulevard, where my sister Joanne was a bookkeeper and connected me with the person responsible for taking on part-time help.

I worked a couple of days a week after school and some Saturdays. My job was to insert metal strips into the spines of books, to prime them for the alarm on the newly installed security system. I was also responsible for gluing covers onto the new hardback books we received. It was basic work, but it gave me some money of my own for the first time in my life. Our parents had never had enough money to give us an allowance, and they figured that chores needed to be done just because you were part of the family, not for reward.

Having gone without any cash in my pocket for so long, I didn't feel the need to spend it just because I now had some. I'd occasionally treat myself to a slice of pizza and a soda on the way home from the library. I also paid to take part in some rec sports leagues for the first time.

If I had one indulgence, it was clothes. Having relied on secondhand purchases and hand-me-downs for years, it was good to be able to buy just what I wanted. I'd picked up a quiet taste for style from Michael, my oldest brother, ten years my senior. He loved to dress well: sharp jeans, silk shirts, alligator shoes. He looked so cool.

I didn't go quite as striking in my style, but I liked to look and feel crisp. When I was growing up, my parents had always said that you didn't have to have a lot of money to look clean and tidy. I agreed. While most of the other students at Jamaica High opted for T-shirts and jeans, I chose slacks and a golf shirt, or a shirt and a tie. One year I was voted best dressed in school and was asked to be photographed for the school yearbook in the full-length cream-colored winter coat I had bought with some of my earnings.

My aim wasn't to stand out, though. I just wanted to dress like I was heading somewhere, to match my clothes to the focus I gave to my schoolwork. Sometimes the other kids would tease me, but I didn't care. I was more motivated by what my parents thought.

Though I started to be given some more freedom, I still put school first. While my siblings would usually put off their home-work until the last minute, it was always the first thing I did when I got home, before anything else. I liked getting things done, and I figured that doing homework or studying straightaway still gave me time to do more before the assignment was due or before the test date, if I wanted to. I knew that good preparation was half the battle.

Once I had finished with band, I didn't get to share much classroom time with Brenda, but I did see her around the school and we would stop and talk. Sometimes I would see her after school, and we would chat before she left; she rode the bus from Springfield Gardens, another part of Queens about twenty min-utes away, slightly more upscale than my Jamaica neighborhood. As the more outgoing of the two of us, she would usually carry the conversation, but over time she taught me to be comfort-able talking more. We exchanged phone numbers, and soon we were often chatting in the evenings about what had happened at school, about movies and music.

We both knew that dating was still out of the question—I'd

learned that in addition to sharing the same last name, our families were similar in other ways; hers was also quite conservative, and religious to a greater degree—but we were getting closer to each other. As we did, my naïveté got me into trouble with her a couple of times.

On one occasion, two or three girls I knew in my humanities class asked whether I wanted to go see a movie with them that night. I agreed and went along innocently, as far as I was concerned; this was just a group of us going out. But apparently there was some ulterior motive behind it all, something to do with that stuff that goes on between girls that I did not understand. Because word got around pretty quickly.

The next day, Brenda stopped me at school. "Hey, I heard you went to the movies last night." I could tell it was more of a question than a statement. I told her what had happened, how I thought that it was just a group outing, innocent stuff.

Brenda explained that the girls had been interested in me, and this was their way of making a statement to everyone else— her included. And she made it plain that she wasn't happy about my accepting the invitation. I apologized, though I was left scratching my head.

I should have learned my lesson, but there was another error in judgment on my part before the lesson finally sank in. Another girl asked me if I wanted to go on a day trip to an amusement park in Pennsylvania. A group of about thirty kids was going, so I didn't think anything about it, and accepted. We hung out together while we were there, and I won her a stuffed animal at one of the stalls. Again, I didn't give this any weight; we were just having a fun day as far as I was concerned. But when Brenda spelled out to me later that there was more going on, I resolved never to get myself into a misunderstanding again.

Besides, I was interested only in Brenda. Since first spotting her and getting to know her, I had discovered that not only was she attractive on the outside; she had a beautiful personality, too. She respected her parents. She was bright—diligent in school, with plans to become a nurse. She was courteous and kind and caring. She more than matched the criteria Mom had given me: "You have got to find someone who is nice and smart." Brenda was both, in buckets, and much more besides.

We officially started dating in eleventh grade. By this stage we'd each visited the other's home and gotten to know the other's parents, among whom there was mutual approval of the match. Developing a relationship with Brenda changed the course of my life in two major ways.

First, it somewhat deepened my faith. I was still going to St. Benedict's every Sunday, but mostly out of obligation. I'd go to one of the early services so I could get it over with and have the rest of the day free. If you had asked me whether I believed in God, I would have said yes, but it was all rather remote. There was head knowledge, but not a lot of heart involved.

Brenda's family was Baptist. She and her older sister, Michele, and mother were devoted members of the famed Cornerstone Baptist Church in Brooklyn. They had attended when they previously lived in the borough, and they continued to return after they had moved away to a better neighborhood.

Brenda's father, George, worked for the transit authority like my dad, but as a motorman. He didn't attend church regularly but was a quiet, strong influence in the home and very protective of his girls.

It could be up to an hour's drive from Brenda's home in Springfield Gardens to Cornerstone, depending on the traffic, but that did not stop them from being there every weekend and sometimes during the week as well for special events.

Together with her mom, Brenda served as an usher and looked as cute as could be in her uniform, with white gloves and stockings. I got to see her dressed to serve when I began to accompany them on Sundays. They had a car—which, together with their address, set them in a higher income bracket than my family was in—and would swing by to pick me up. Sometimes I would ride the bus twenty minutes over to their house to catch a ride.

Cornerstone was a world away from St. Benedict's. For starters, it dwarfed my Catholic church home. The ground level alone was bigger than St. Benedict's, but then there was a second-level tier of seating rising high, almost like in a theater. And the place would be packed, with up to ten times the number at St. Benedict's. Then, when the members of the choir opened their mouths, oh my. The music was amazing. It was exuberant and alive and joyful, apparently coming from somewhere deep inside each singer. We sang at St. Benedict's, but nothing like this; ours was much more dutiful and subdued. At Cornerstone, I half wondered whether the roof might get blown off by the gusto.

The services lasted much longer, too, but I didn't find myself watching the clock. I was caught up by the stirring preaching. The homilies at St. Benedict's were thoughtful—when I bothered to tune in—but at Cornerstone they were delivered with a passion and a touch of theater that almost insisted you listen and listen good. I'd heard about God at St. Benedict's, but at Cornerstone I began to hear more about Jesus, about how He came to earth to save us from our sins and give us a new life, which was something to celebrate.

Sunday morning's eleven o'clock service at Cornerstone would often run a couple of hours, and even then church wasn't over. People would then take time to visit with one another. "Hey, Sister Louise," someone would call out to Brenda's mother. "How are you doing?" I'd always be introduced and made to feel welcome. Often, by the time we had finished visiting and made the drive back home it would be three p.m. or later.

As we'd set out for church at about ten a.m., it meant that much of Sunday was given over to church, but I did not mind. I was with Brenda, and I was having my faith stretched and stirred. I realized that while I had known something about God from my time at St. Benedict's, for the first time I was beginning to sense that there was more, that I could actually know Him personally.

I still attended St. Benedict's from time to time—on occasion Brenda would go there with me—and Mom didn't seem to mind about my gradual switch of affiliation. She was just glad that I was attending church with some greater apparent enthusiasm, and she liked that I was spending time with such a good, faith-centered family.

In addition to playing a significant part in shaping my religious beliefs, Brenda was also instrumental in shaping my future. Though I was doing very well in high school, I hadn't really given any thought to what might happen afterward. Apart from some of my siblings, who had taken a few college courses but soon gave up on the idea of further education, no one in my family had ever gone on to college. Academic abilities aside, there was the question of money. It simply wasn't something my family could afford.

Teachers had encouraged me along the way, telling me that I might make something of myself, starting with Mrs. Wright.

Then there had been Mr. Kaufman, my homeroom and social studies teacher at I.S. 8. He would tell me, "Mark, you've got something special. You could do anything you want."

But I didn't start to even consider the idea of taking my schooling further until Brenda and I began talking about life after Jamaica High. She was going to follow Michele, she told me, and go to college. She wanted to become a nurse.

"What about you, Tony? Where are you going to go?"

I told her that I didn't plan on going to college.

"Whyever not?" Brenda wanted to know. "You should definitely go. You're the smartest person in the room."

Her encouragement made me think seriously for the first time that it might even be a possibility, but it was Dr. Paul, my guidance counselor, who pushed me further.

In my senior year, he asked about my plans. I said I'd probably look for a job and maybe take some further classes in my spare time at City College, which was local and offered evening classes.

"You really need to apply for full-time college, Mark," he said. "Why don't you at least talk to your parents about it?"

It seemed like a waste of time to me, but I agreed and spoke with Mom later that day. I told her that Dr. Paul thought I should think about going on to college. She said that I needed to ask Dad about it.

When I did, he was dismissive. "College? Son, I can't afford college. You're number seven of eight kids. You know that. We don't have the money for college."

His response didn't upset me too much, because it didn't really surprise me, but it made Dr. Paul raise his eyebrows when I told him. He encouraged me to go back and ask one more time. Something was stirring in me about the idea of getting a degree, so I agreed. This time, I went straight to my father.

"Dad, I told Dr. Paul what you said, and he really thinks that I need to go to college. And, Dad, I'd really like to do that. Now, I know you said no, but Dr. Paul wanted me to ask you again. Could you reconsider and allow me to go to college?"

There was a moment's silence. "Okay, son," he said simply. "I don't know how we are going to do it, but we will find a way to send you to college. We'll figure it out."

His agreement wasn't an open ticket, however. Brenda had her sights set far afield—she was talking about applying to Temple University in Philadelphia, both because it had a great reputation and also because it was out of state; she wanted to experience life beyond New York. I knew that my family's financial limitations would restrict me to an in-state school, where the costs would be much less.

I also knew what I wanted to study. Because I had done advanced classes back in junior high, by the time I began my senior year at Jamaica High I had already completed my required math studies. I got to choose from several electives, including accounting. I didn't know much about it, other than my sister Joanne was part of that world, as a bookkeeper at the library. I signed up, and I loved it from the get-go.

Some of the other students really struggled, but for me there was a logic and clarity about it all that I found fascinating. I enjoyed working with the columns of debits and credits and having to reconcile the two. It was a kind of language of its own. I finished the class with an A, then signed up for a second, more advanced accounting class, which I also aced.

During this whole time, Brenda and I were also growing ever

closer. Our first official date had been in May 1977. I rode over by bus and picked her up, and we went to the Sunrise movie theater in Valley Stream, Long Island, to see a new sci-fi adventure that was getting a lot of buzz: *Star Wars*.

If Brenda had been helpful in encouraging me to pursue my academic education, she had also made an important contribution to my social education. Drawing me out in conversation, pulling me from my shy shell, was the first step. The next involved putting my thoughts and feelings down on paper.

One day in school, before we were formally "a couple," she pressed something into my hand as we passed in the hall. It was a handwritten note, telling me what she was thinking and feeling. I liked having her tangible expression to hold, and I wrote a note back. Soon we were exchanging notes regularly, somehow finding it a little easier to be open and honest about our emotions and hopes and dreams on paper than in person.

Overcoming my shyness was a process. We graduated to holding hands—at her initiation—as we'd sit together in the basement at Brenda's home, listening to music or watching the black-and-white television. Her mother or father would come down from time to time, ostensibly to fetch something, but we all knew they really did it to keep an eye on us. Not that we were up to anything untoward: the imprint of my parents' protectiveness combined with my sense of what was proper and my lack of confidence meant that I was not going to try anything. I didn't view Brenda the way a lot of the other guys at high school did their girlfriends, someone to try to take advantage of.

But there can be a fine line between being courteous and being chicken. Finally, one night, as we sat together, Brenda took my hand and said, "You know, Tony, it's okay to kiss me."

Having never kissed a girl before, I must have looked shocked or worried. Thankfully, she took the lead and showed me how. It was very sweet. As we broke, I asked with a smile, "How do you know how to do this?"

Brenda chuckled and shrugged. "I have no idea." I was happy to study further with her.

CHAPTER 5

"YOU'VE JUST MISSED HER"

When kids head off to college, people talk about them going out into the big, wide world. That was certainly true for me: before leaving high school I had been out of New York City only twice.

Once my family had gone to the beach at Montauk, on Long Island, for a couple of days with friends who owned an RV. My biggest trip was at age twelve or so, when Mom took Gary and me down to South Carolina to meet some of our extended family.

Granddad's house, her father's, was really way out in the country, sitting all alone at the end of a single-lane road. There were no streetlights, so at night it was pitch black. It was neat to be able to see the stars so clearly, but all the unfamiliar wildlife sounds spooked me. I felt safer back in the city, amid all the urban noise I was used to.

Granddad invited me to help collect the eggs from the chicken coop in the morning. He probably thought it would be fun, but I declined. The idea of having to contend with all the clucking birds and mess did not appeal at all; I preferred picking my eggs from the grocery store shelf, nicely gathered in a tidy box.

My options for college were restricted by our financial limitations to in-state schools. Of those, only the University of Buffalo offered the accounting major I was interested in. Though Brenda had one eye on Temple, she also wanted to check out the nursing program at Buffalo, which had its own strong reputation.

We made a discovery trip together, with her parents. I was blown away by the campus and the city. There seemed to be so much open space and green, a marked contrast to the concrete and asphalt of Queens. I was sold—and then delighted when Brenda decided that Buffalo was where she wanted to go, too. We were already committed to each other and had planned on continuing our relationship long-distance if she headed to Pennsylvania, but experiencing college together would be even better.

College proved to be a bit of a testing ground. The straight-A student learned that he was going to have to step up his game if he wanted to stay at the front of the pack. The classes and the faculty were way more demanding.

But the adjustments weren't merely academic. I was finding my way into a bigger world beyond my parents' protective oversight, and having kept a year ahead through the rest of high school after starting there as a tenth grader, I was only seventeen when I arrived at the largest university in the New York State system.

That helps explain my one bad experience with alcohol. I had turned eighteen, then the legal drinking age, when I went to a local bar with some other students to watch a hockey game. So I was breaking only my parents' rule, not the law.

We ordered some Buffalo wings, naturally, and a pitcher of beer. I decided to try it. The taste was okay, but I didn't really see why so many people raved about the stuff. Eating wings and watching the game, I kept sipping, overlooking the fact that someone kept topping off all the glasses.

When it came time to leave, a couple of hours later, I realized something was wrong. My legs felt sleepy and did not want to cooperate with my brain. When I eventually got back to my room, I was as sick as a dog. I woke up the next morning lying on the bathroom tiles, with my arms wrapped around the porcelain stand of the toilet. Never again.

Other learning curves included getting along with people from very different backgrounds. Growing up in Jamaica, Queens, had taught me to stay on my toes and have my radar screen up, but that had all been within a familiar African American context.

My first accommodations at Buffalo were with three other guys—all white—in a room for three. Tight quarters were nothing new to me, of course, but living in such close proximity made me aware of how different our backgrounds and perspectives were. I was too caught off guard to be offended when one of my roommates asked to touch my Afro because he wanted to know what black hair felt like. I did think that maybe I should ask to touch his for the same reason, though.

In due course, one of the other three guys was slated to move to different accommodations, but I went to the housing officer and requested to be relocated instead. Not so much because I was uncomfortable, but because clearly the three of them were a better fit.

The move wasn't a good one, however. There were only three of us in the new room, but both of the others were mature students in their midtwenties, meaning there was quite an age gap. Additionally, one of them, Brad, described himself as a recovering alcoholic but spent most of his spare time getting drunk. The other was Mohamed, an African Muslim who insisted on rearranging the furniture in the room so he could stretch out his prayer mat in the direction of Mecca several times a day, and wanted us all to take off our shoes before entering the room as a mark of religious respect. Despite his apparent spiritual fervor, he also smoked marijuana regularly.

The two of them clashed frequently. One time I came back to the aftermath of a big fight, with holes in the wall and things overturned. It was all rather intimidating, but I kept up my guard and made a lot of the fact that I was from New York City, man, hoping they would think better than to mess with someone from such a tough environment.

When the situation didn't improve, I told Mom and Dad about how hard things were, in one of my weekly Sunday afternoon calls home. The next thing I knew, I was being pulled out of class one day and told to go to the housing office. There I was informed that I was being moved immediately, and I ended up sharing a two-person room with an easygoing Asian student.

Later I learned that Dad had stepped in to help. Hearing how tough my situation was, he had called the housing office to demand a transfer. The housing administrator explained that there was nothing they could do; in fact, I'd been the one to choose to leave my previous room situation, they pointed out. Maybe so, he said, but my new accommodations were not acceptable and they needed to sort something out for his son, or he would be coming up to Buffalo for a "discussion" about it.

Knowing that my parents still had my back, even from a distance, was a real encouragement as I continued to adjust to life away from them. But there was nothing they could do to protect me from the events that plunged me into my most challenging days as a student. For a season, whether I would make it through seemed a touch-and-go proposition.

Mom first got sick when I was thirteen. Breast cancer. She underwent a double mastectomy and radiation therapy. The doctors said that if she got through five years, she would be in the clear.

Mom and Dad didn't talk about it a lot, probably wanting to shield us from the worry, and at that age I wasn't aware how serious her illness was. All I knew was that after the surgery we had to take care of some of the many things she had done for us all that we had taken for granted. She couldn't cook, wash the clothes, or clean the house, so our chores list got longer. Family and friends helped out, bringing some meals by, and we ate a lot more cold cuts than we used to. But by the time I set off for Buffalo, her illness was a fading memory for me.

Because money was tight and Buffalo was a ten-hour drive from New York City, I didn't get home to visit during the semester. Our contact was limited to my Sunday calls.

The first time Mom didn't come to the phone, sometime around March of my freshman year, I didn't think anything of it. When I asked to talk to her, one of my sisters just said that she was out. That was unusual because she was pretty much always home, but maybe she was out visiting a friend. When I was told the same thing the next week, I knew that something was up. What was wrong? I insisted on knowing.

She was in the hospital.

"Your mother is sick again, son," Dad told me. "The cancer is back." I pushed for more details, but he and my sisters were vague. The cancer had metastasized, they said, but she was getting further treatment. She was in the hospital for a few days at a time; then she was allowed home again for a while. Everyone was hoping for the best.

It was a relief when spring semester ended and Brenda and I headed back to New York City, so I could be closer. I got a job at the library where I had worked before, which helped me meet my school costs. When she was at home, Brenda went around during the day to take care of Mom, getting to use some of the nursing training she was receiving. When Mom was in Mary Immaculate Hospital, I'd walk down there to visit her during my lunch hour, buying a sandwich in the hospital cafeteria and eating it in her room as we chatted.

She had lost some weight, but she always tried to be bright and cheerful, asking me about school and encouraging me to do my best. One day I told her that I was thinking about seeing whether I could transfer from Buffalo to St. John's University, a Catholic school with a campus in Queens. I didn't know how I would pay for it, but I would work something out. Most important, it would mean I could be around to see her and help out.

"No, you're not," she said with that definite tone of hers that meant there was to be no arguing.

"There's no reason for you to come back here to be near me," she went on. "There's nothing you can do for me here. I'm being well cared for, and you need to be in Buffalo, Mark. I just need you to do two things. Be nice to Brenda, and look out for your younger brother."

I told her I would do both those things, acknowledging her affection for Brenda and her concern for Gary, who was struggling after getting sucked in by some bad influences in the neighborhood. I didn't realize that she was also telling me good-bye.

I was in my regular place in the lecture hall along with some two hundred other Buffalo students—down in the front row, so I could concentrate—on the morning of November 2, 1979, when a campus security officer came in and interrupted the professor. "Is there a Mark Moore here?"

I followed him out of the room with everyone looking at me, aware they probably thought I was in trouble for something. "What's the matter?" I asked, knowing I hadn't done anything wrong.

Out in the hallway, the officer told me, "I need you to call home right away. Your family called, and they need to speak with you."

I still wasn't thinking this was related to Mom. Maybe it was Gary. Or perhaps someone had been in an accident.

"Mark," Rochelle said when I called. "Mom is really, really sick. You need to come home right now."

"You mean, like, right now? Today?"

"Yes, Mark," she said. "Just get on the first plane you can."

The reality of the situation flooded me. I immediately turned to Brenda. We had copies of each other's class schedules, so I knew where she was. I went over there and found her.

"Bren, the family called. Mom's really sick, and I have to get home."

She rose without hesitation. "I'm coming with you."

We called her parents to explain what was happening. They told us to get on the first flight to LaGuardia that we could—they'd take care of the tickets—and someone would be there to meet us in their car and take us to the hospital. Racing to Buffalo airport, we managed to get seats on a flight within two or three hours and were back in New York City by late afternoon. Michele and Clarence were waiting at LaGuardia for us and drove us straight to Mary Immaculate Hospital.

I sensed it as soon as we got off the elevator on Mom's floor. Something was wrong; there was a huddle of family outside her room, not in there with her. Seeing us, someone came over. "I'm sorry," they told me. "She waited as long as she could, Mark. You've just missed her."

I was heartbroken. I went into her room for a private moment with her. I got to kiss her cheek and tell her that I loved her. The family told me that she had been asking for me by name right up until she passed. As upsetting as it was to hear, I also found it strangely comforting in a way. I thought back to our final conversation, before I'd returned to Buffalo, and realized how she had been expressing her love for me, not wanting her death to interfere with my life. As painful as it was, Mom's passing also further cemented Brenda's place in my life and in our family. When we gathered at the house on the day of the funeral, things got a bit heated when it came to deciding who would ride with us in the family car to St. Benedict the Moor for the funeral service and then on to Calverton National Cemetery for military families in Riverhead, Long Island, for the burial. Emotions were raw and running high, and not everyone was happy about the seating arrangements for partners. It was tense and awkward.

"This is my house and that is my wife," Dad declared with finality. "Brenda is in the family car," he went on, tacitly acknowledging how she had been the one to feed, bathe, and care for Mom so much when we were back during the summer—just like a daughter. "Discussion over."

Mom's death sent me into a real tailspin. While I had never coasted at school, always being diligent and doing my best, since arriving at university I'd had to up my game to keep pace. But now with the weight of loss adding to the pressures of the course work, I was really floundering in class. I started getting Cs and Ds in my classes. I doubled down and tried even harder, but it didn't seem to make any difference. What had been doable, if not easy, was now a constant struggle, like I was suddenly running with weights around my ankles.

I did not recognize it at the time, but I was most likely suffering from depression. It did not occur to me to seek help by going to the student health clinic. Sadly, nor did my difficulties drive me deeper into faith.

Belief was certainly much more meaningful for me now, having experienced Cornerstone Baptist Church, than it had been previously, and Brenda and I continued to attend church faithfully each Sunday, even though we were now far beyond the watchful eyes of our mothers. We found a Presbyterian church that attracted a number of other students. But faith was still something that I restricted to Sunday mornings, taking the reins back for the rest of the week. The idea that God could be an active part of all of my life outside the walls of church was still a foreign concept.

Those gray days of loss were further darkened by the challenge of making ends meet. Even with my parents' support, some financial breaks from the university, and my summer job, money was really tight. I got a work-study job on campus, which put me back in the library, fixing metal security tabs to books once again. I also became the treasurer of the student government, which brought in a little extra money and also gave me some early experience of management and leadership and working with others in organizations.

Yet there always seemed to be more month than money. My greatest asset was a small toaster oven that allowed me to make grilled cheese sandwiches in my room. Two slices of bread and some cheese, and I had yet another meal to wash down with water. Meals at home in Jamaica, Queens, hadn't been lavish, but sometimes they seemed like banquets when compared to yet another grilled cheese sandwich.

At one stage, money was so short that Brenda and I were forced to pawn our high school rings. We'd exchanged them not long after we began dating, each wearing the other's as a sort of unofficial, just-between-us engagement ring. Though the rings meant a lot to us, selling them was just something we had to do.

We got engaged over Christmas of our junior year. We had been talking about it since not long after we first started dating, at first in the vague way of young love but more concretely as time went by. We knew that we wanted to be together, we knew that we wanted to have children, and we knew that we wanted to make a good life for ourselves through our respective careers.

I managed to save up a couple of hundred dollars—a fortune, given my limited means—for a ring, and I went down on one knee at Brenda's home. Everyone was very happy for us. We told them we planned to finish school before getting married and settling down.

My love for Brenda had been further deepened by her care and support during the eighteen months or so I was having a hard time after Mom's death. Eventually things turned around and I found my old sense of confidence in my studies. My grades began to come back up. Brenda was a large part of that recovery, encouraging me to keep going, telling me that I could do it, that she believed in me, reminding me that I had what it took.

If the hard times I faced in Buffalo were further evidence— not that I needed it—that Brenda was the one I wanted to have a family with, they also reminded me of how fortunate I was to come from the family I did.

Not long after I returned to Buffalo following Mom's death, Dad had some more challenging news.

"Son, I've got a lot of extra bills to pay," he explained. "Your mother was in the hospital on and off for something like eight months, and the insurance covers only so much. I don't know how much money I am going to be able to keep sending you." I could sense the regret in his voice, as he had committed to making it possible for me to go to school. I knew that he had always prided himself on being a man of his word.

"Don't worry, Dad," I told him. "I understand. It's okay. I will work something out."

But it wasn't, and I didn't really know what to do. Even working two jobs and surviving on grilled cheese wasn't cutting it.

Then, one day, a chunky envelope arrived in the mail. There was a note from Rochelle.

Hi, Mark. Here's some money we all want you to have to help you get through college.

Wrapped in white paper was a bundle of different bills, totaling several hundred dollars. I was floored. None of my brothers or sisters had been able to pursue further education to try to make more of themselves, for one reason or another. They were working hard, doing the best they could, and yet they wanted to make sure that I did not miss out on my opportunity for more. They were sacrificing so that I could stay in school.

Mom might not have been with us anymore in person, but she was still there in spirit, her children honoring her number one concern, that we keep looking out for one another, because we were family. My siblings' gift not only made a big practical difference; it also helped lift my spirits and inspired me to redouble my efforts. Not only did I not want to let myself or my parents down; I did not want to waste my brothers' and sisters' investment.

That and similar cash donations that would arrive from time to time were not the only generosity I experienced from family. None of us kids had learned to drive while we were growing up. We didn't have the money, but neither did we have the need; you could get around pretty well by public transport in New York City. Brenda and I got our driver's licenses while we were in Buffalo.

Meanwhile, Donna had bought a car back in Jamaica. Still living at home, she worked an administrative job in the New York City hospital system. Someone she knew who worked there sold her an old car, a big, brown Mercury Marquis. She planned on getting her license, but the vehicle ended up sitting outside the house unused for months. Eventually, she said, "Mark, you've got your license. Why don't you just take it?"

I was hugely grateful, of course. But if the car was a gift horse, it was also an old nag destined for the knacker's yard—doubtless why Donna's coworker had been eager to offload it on her. I didn't look it in the mouth, but I spent a fair amount of time under the hood, checking the oil level. There was some sort of problem that meant it guzzled oil, along with gas, so I would buy a box of refill oil cans and stash them in the trunk, pulling over to the side of the road at regular intervals to top up the level.

This was just a minor expense and inconvenience compared to the advantages, however. It made life much easier for Brenda and me as we juggled classes and schedules on different parts of the large campus. It drove like a boat, all billowy, but we were as thrilled as we could be as we cruised along, typically with Marvin Gaye's "What's Going On" cranked on the eight track and half an eye on the oil gauge.

Occasionally we would dare to take it farther afield. We visited Brenda's cousin and his family, living near Rochester, about an hour from Buffalo. We also went up there to try skiing for the first time. I hadn't enjoyed the winters I had experienced while in school—it had been spring when I visited the campus, so the bitter cold that came a few months later caught me completely by surprise—but I came to appreciate them more when we got onto the slopes. It was a big kick for me, a New York City kid, to be out there on skis.

If there had been a valley during my time at Buffalo, I was coming up the other side by the time I graduated with a bachelor of science in accounting, a few months before Brenda earned her bachelor's in nursing. Some of my peers had long-term plans for what they wanted to do after graduation, but it wasn't until my final year that I began to wonder what might be next for me.

My academic adviser suggested I submit my transcripts to what were then the Big Eight accounting firms when they came to campus looking for new talent. I didn't really understand how significant these companies were, but I figured I might as well apply, and I ended up with interviews with six of them.

If I had known more about the financial world, I might have been more impressed, or maybe more intimidated. As it was, when the first offer of a position came with a twenty-five-thousand-dollar annual starting salary and, more important, a position in the New York City office that would allow me to move back closer to my family, it seemed too good an offer to pass up.

CHAPTER 6

"SOMEONE I CAN RELY ON"

I thought of Cousin Don as I walked along Sixth Avenue with a new brown briefcase firmly in my right hand. I was slightly nervous but also excited as I arrived at the front door of the Manhattan offices of Arthur Andersen LLC.

Some thirty years later, the Chicago area–based firm's reputation would be left in tatters in the wake of the Enron financial scandal, in which it was discovered that the company's energy-giant client had hidden billions of dollars in debt. But when I reported for my first day in June 1982, Arthur Andersen was yet ranked among the nation's most elite accounting firms.

Securing a position there was something of a coup, with strong competition for one of the entry-level places. Only a handful of the fifteen hundred or so employees at the New York City offices were African American, so I stood out a bit. And not only because of the color of my skin.

Though I always tried to dress well, I had taken extra care before I set out that morning. I'd chosen one of my best church outfits: a double-breasted navy blue blazer and gray slacks, with a blue tie over a white shirt. I thought it was stylishly subdued. Not so much.

At one point during the day, one of the other new guys in the office, an older man, came over. "Hey," he said, his manner friendly. "You may want to buy a suit, you know."

I was a bit taken aback. "What do you mean?" I said, brushing my tie and looking down at my clothes to check that everything matched well.

"They don't want people dressing like that," the man told me. "Too casual. They like suits. More conservative. More businesslike. You're going to need to get yourself a suit."

I thanked him for the heads-up. That evening I went to a department store and purchased three suits: blue, black, and dark gray. I'd wear a suit to the office every single working day of my life after that.

The wardrobe lesson wasn't the only indicator that first day that I was entering a new world about which I knew little. As I started to gather my things together in readiness for leaving around five p.m., someone sitting near me looked over.

"What ya doing?"

"Getting ready to leave."

"We don't go home at five."

"We don't?"

"No. We just work until it's done."

I put my new briefcase down again, although I didn't actually have anything else to do after just nine hours in the job. That would soon change, and along with a new wardrobe I embraced a different work ethic, which would routinely see me among the last to leave.

Life at Arthur Andersen was certainly demanding, but

I loved it and rose to the challenge. While I might have been new to the business world, I was soon thrown into the deep end. They assigned me to auditing teams that handled big projects like Merck & Co. pharmaceuticals and United Artists. These audits took us away from our Arthur Andersen desks to sites around the city and farther afield, sometimes for weeks at a time. I learned that you didn't want to spend much time back at the office in Manhattan; if you were there, it meant the boss didn't trust you to be sent out on a job.

I loved the auditing process, which involved more than just the accounting practices I had learned in Buffalo. You had to not only read the financial reports accurately, but then interpret them, taking data and turning it into smart business decisions. Is this a good investment? Where are the costs out of line? I discovered that I had a gift for not only reading the lines in the different columns, but also reading between the lines, as it were.

There was only one cloud in my sunny skies, and that was on the home front.

I had graduated from Buffalo six months ahead of Brenda and moved back to New York City to start work at Arthur Andersen. I stayed with her parents for the first six months, an indication of how close I had grown to them. They had accepted me from the start of my relationship with Brenda, even though they might have been forgiven for having reservations about this young man who was from a slightly less desirable part of the city but who was interested in their daughter. Like Brenda, they encouraged me to pursue my education, telling me I had potential. They were kind and generous.

When Mom died, Brenda's mother had told me, "No one can ever replace your mom, Mark, but I'm here for you, if you need me." I did, and I would call her Mom in due course. Brenda's father was quiet, especially in contrast to my father, who loved to talk, but when he spoke I knew he had something important to say, and I always felt at ease talking with him.

I found an apartment that would be Brenda's and my first home together, the upper level of a converted house in Cambria Heights, Queens—another step up for me from Jamaica. We moved in there after marrying at Cornerstone Baptist Church on July 3, 1983.

Life was good. I was married at last to my high school sweetheart, and we soon discovered that we were expecting our first child. We were surprised by how quickly Brenda became pregnant, but not disappointed; we'd already talked about wanting children and not wanting to wait too long for them. Losing my mother at just forty-eight years of age had underscored for us that you never know how life might change, and we felt it wasn't wise to put things off to a future that you might not have.

We were trying to juggle the implications of new parenthood with the demands both our fledgling careers were making. On graduation, Brenda had secured a spot in her preferred specialty, obstetrics and gynecology, at North Shore University Hospital in Manhasset, Long Island. She was delighted to be working with moms and their newborns, but the only position available was on the less-favored night shift.

This meant that we were often ships in the night. I was routinely clocking long days at Arthur Andersen, arriving at the office or my audit location by seven thirty in the morning and often not leaving until at least twelve hours later. I had learned soon after arriving that if you were logging only forty billable hours of work a week, you were considered a slacker.

I didn't mind working long and hard—doing so tapped into my own personality and determination, the lessons my parents had drilled into me, and a sliver of awareness that as very much a minority in a white workplace, I needed to work that bit more to get ahead.

As a result, though, I would typically get home just in time to trade a few words and a kiss with Brenda before she had to head out for her shift. Thankfully, we were close enough to family members so they could help out after Jenée arrived on April 25, 1984. But we both knew that something was going to have to change for the long haul.

The opportunity came with Radio Relay, a division of Graphics Scanning Corporation, based in Plainview, Long Island. This part of the company was in the pager business. Cell phone technology was still in its infancy: "mobile" phones were large, clunky things as big as bricks, attached to a transceiver that had to be carried in a backpack. And if that wasn't off-putting enough, they cost a fortune to use. So most people used pagers.

Radio Relay was looking for a senior accountant, and the recruiter was delighted to receive an application from someone at Arthur Andersen: that name put your résumé at the top of the pile.

I found myself advancing pretty quickly. When the company relocated operations to Englewood, New Jersey, I went there as controller. Only a year or so later, Stan Sech, the general manager of the division I oversaw, came into my office one day. He told me that he had been hired as chief executive officer for USA Mobile Communications, a communications start-up company in Cincinnati, Ohio. He wanted me to join him as his chief financial officer.

I was flattered, but also rather surprised, and I told him so. There were two people in senior financial positions, vice presidents, between me and Stan; what about either of them?

"I'll be honest with you, Mark," he said. "It's because I know that you do the work. A lot of these reports that come to meetings, they may not have your name on them, but you're the one responsible for them. You don't mind hard work, and this start-up is going to be hard work, lots of it. I need someone like you, someone I can rely on." The offer was tempting, but it also needed thinking through carefully. I was glad to be out of Jamaica, Queens, but I had not really thought seriously about moving much farther afield. I was still a New York City boy at heart. Brenda and I both remained close to our families, and we were glad that Jenée was near her grandparents. The area we were living in was a good one for raising children. Our faith was still pretty compartmentalized, but we attended Cornerstone whenever we could, work and other commitments allowing. It would take something pretty special for us to consider uprooting.

At the same time, Stan was presenting me with a big opportunity. This was a ground-floor open door in a business with huge potential, not only for financial reward but also for business experience. Brenda and I made an exploratory visit to Cincinnati. We liked what we saw and experienced of the quality of life there.

Careerwise, the move would be a risk, but a calculated one. I knew enough about business by now not to be foolhardy. Evaluating all the factors, I concluded that I was confident in the three core Ms that mattered when it came to making a decision: the market, the management, and myself.

I believed communication technology was the cutting-edge place to be. I knew Stan to be a good leader. I was fairly sure that I could handle whatever I was given. And if worse came to worst, what had I really lost? I was still young, and I had some good connections that could surely help me find another opportunity.

Having decided to make the move, I then learned another important business lesson: even when you have done your due diligence, you will never fully know what you are getting yourself into. And, chances are, things will be tougher than you expected.

USA Mobile had been created by investors who purchased several different Cincinnati Bell properties with telephone, mobile, and cell interests. Our job was to take these different threads and weave them into a cohesive new operation.

We were actually the second team to be assembled for the project. The first group lasted only nine months before being let go. When Stan was tapped to lead another attempt to make USA Mobile fly, he recruited me and another Radio Relay colleague as chief technology officer.

What I had believed from my research to have been a bit of a muddle turned out to be a complete mess, I found once I arrived in Cincinnati. Operations were in chaos, while accounting was even worse. Financial statements hadn't been prepared in months. We all rolled our sleeves up and dug in, knowing the make or break lay in our hands. It was exciting and scary at the same time, but I was energized by the sense of mission that we shared.

Key to the progress we were able to make was sticking to our strategy. We had a plan and we worked it. Part of our approach was to be low-key. We needed to expand through other acquisitions, but we chose to avoid the crowded and high-profile markets of the West and East Coasts. From Cincinnati we expanded to Dayton and Cleveland, then in stages into Kentucky, Alabama, Tennessee, Illinois, and Missouri.

I was on the road a lot, visiting our different offices. Reading the reports back at my desk in Cincinnati could tell me only so much. Spending time in our different locations, I audited cash, inventory, and receivables. As I did, I began to see more clearly what was behind some of the numbers.

We had all sorts of problems with staff embezzling. Because cash payments were still quite common at this time, ahead of more widespread use of credit cards, it was rather easy to misdirect some of the money between the customer's pocket and USA Mobile's account. If someone brought in fifty dollars to make a payment, an employee might take it, make a credit adjustment in the customer's account for that amount in the computer system, then pocket the bills. The customer's account showed no delinquency, but the money never made it into the company's coffers. We also had a major problem with inventory going missing.

I instituted new systems that closed the loopholes. Three-way tying helped. You could make A and B look like they reconciled, even if they didn't, fairly easily, or do the same with B and C. But insisting that A and B and C all line up made it much harder to hide inconsistencies. So I checked cash receipt records against bank deposits and then against credits posted to clients' accounts. I also required hand counts of all stock. As well as tightening up on operations, I also had to let quite a few people go. It was not something I enjoyed, but at the end of the day they were stealing, and that could not be allowed to continue if we were to remain in business—not just for ourselves, but for all the other employees and the investors, too.

Within a short time we were starting to see operations come together. The investors were relieved. They told us so at a dinner at Morton's, a wonderful steakhouse in downtown Cincinnati. "We're really glad you guys are here," one of the backers told me as we chatted informally, revealing just how precarious a situation we had accepted. "Actually, if we hadn't been able to hire Stan and you, we were going to shut this thing down."

Four years in Cincinnati went by pretty quickly. Brenda and I were delighted to welcome our son, Markus, into the world on January 29, 1992. Family life was good. We attended church most Sundays, but that continued to be about the extent of our involvement. USA Mobile took up the bulk of my week, but we were starting to see a return on our long hours of investment. The business had grown steadily, to the point where it was ready to be taken public, as the investors had wanted all along.

This process further extended my boundaries—and tested my principles. I was moving beyond helping run a business successfully into entrepreneurial territory, from ensuring that the business we had was efficient and effective to imagining what might be.

As part of the initial public offering, I was offered some stock options. Stan and I were told what was on the table in a meeting from which our chief technology officer was absent; being more on the technical end of things, he often was not involved when we sat down with the investors. But I was surprised to learn that his portion was to be less than mine. I asked why.

"Well, there's the CEO in a company and then behind him there's the CFO, the number two, in effect," I was told. "That's you."

That was the way things worked, I acknowledged, but our CTO had made the same gamble when he left Radio Relay as I had, I thought. His technical contributions had been a crucial part of our success. I told them that I wanted him and me to share the same number of stocks. They agreed to my request but shook their heads a little in disbelief.

I knew I was giving some money away—and in a few months' time we went on to sell the company for around six hundred million dollars—but I didn't bother to calculate how much. As far as I was concerned, it was just the right thing to do. You couldn't put a dollar amount on that.

And though I may have forfeited some money, by this point, in my midthirties, I was moving in circles way beyond anything I could have imagined as a kid back in Jamaica, Queens. As part of the IPO with USA Mobile, I traveled widely, meeting with potential investors across the country and overseas. We stayed at some of the best hotels and ate at some of the best restaurants.

Brenda and I weren't ostentatious, but we were able to enjoy nice things. We had a comfortable but modest home; looking in on our family life from the outside, our suburban neighbors would not have known that we were doing very well financially.

One enjoyable benefit of my success was being able to share it with Dad. He was still in Queens, planning to remarry a few years after Mom had passed. When he and the woman he had been in a relationship with for some time decided to get married at city hall, on the spur of the moment, he called to ask me to be his best man. I was touched, but unfortunately I was away on business and unable to get there on such short notice.

But I did visit New York City fairly regularly to meet with folks on Wall Street, and I'd make a point of carving out time to see my father. I'd stay at a nice hotel in Manhattan, for convenience for business appointments, and send a car to collect him from the house on 171st Street. I got a kick out of being able to take him to some of the best restaurants in town, which he enjoyed.

One night we were eating at Sylvia's, one of Dad's favorites:

the Harlem restaurant is famed for its great soul food. As we reminisced over our meal, I recalled how he had been very strict with us kids. I brought up the time he had grounded me ahead of the basketball final, in junior high.

"I'm not mad with you about it, Dad, but you know, I think you were wrong on that one," I told him.

He looked over at me and grinned. "Is that so?" he said. "So let me be sure I'm getting this right. You're living in a nice house in Cincinnati. You've just come from Wall Street, where you have been meeting with a bunch of investment bankers. We're at Sylvia's. You're sitting there wearing a tailored suit, French cuffs, and cuff links, and now you're going to tell me I made a mistake?" He grinned.

He had a point: I could only chuckle. "You know what? Never mind."

We laughed together; then Dad got serious. "Mark, I hear you," he said. "I'm not going to say I was always right, but I want you to know that I always did what I thought was right."

These dinner outings were one small way I could thank Dad for the way he had shaped and influenced me. I was keenly aware of the significance of my upbringing in preparing me for the opportunities that came my way in business, emphasizing the importance of discipline and determination. Those qualities had been a major part of my successful climb up the career ladder.

One lesson I had yet to learn, however, was the importance of failing well. The class would be in Greenville, South Carolina, where I was recruited from USA Mobile to become chief financial officer at Conxus, another mobile communications start-up.

Pocketalk was a great messaging concept, allowing people to cheaply receive voice mails on their mobile phones, but it took much longer to iron out the development kinks than expected.

By the time those problems were fixed, the communications world had moved on; we were simply too late to market. A further cash injection from investors to try to salvage the project was denied. There would be no more fuel for this flight—the only thing left was to bring it down without too much damage.

I got the job of being at the controls for the crash landing, though it was not one I would have chosen. When the company filed for bankruptcy, the CEO was the first to be let go, followed by our chief operations officer. I figured that I was next in line, but instead I was asked to stay on.

"Bankruptcy is a financial move," I was told. "So we need someone who can handle all that, a CFO. We need you."

So began some of the toughest months of my business career. I had enjoyed one success after another, so being part of a failure left a bitter taste in my mouth, and I didn't like it one bit. But I decided that I was not simply going to walk away. I was going to see this thing out to the best of my abilities. I wanted the negative impact to be as minimal as possible for everyone.

There were hard decisions to make. We needed only a skeleton crew to carry the process through to the end. That meant letting lots of people go—among them colleagues who had become friends.

Much as I disliked the tension, I didn't shirk my responsibilities. I decided that I would not inform anyone that their position was ending by memo or phone call: I would tell them all in person. They deserved that mark of respect, and I wanted to tell them that I appreciated all they had done for the company.

You might think that everyone who was kept on through to the bitter end would have been grateful for the extra time and money. But there were headaches handling those who escaped the cuts. Some started to think they could slack off in their efforts, taking two-hour lunches, for example. I had to be as firm here as I was trying to be fair with those who were leaving.

In addition to handling personnel issues, I needed to double down on our accounting. Every single dollar was going to be scrutinized, so my always-exacting standards had to be raised even higher.

All these internal stresses were matched by external ones of maybe even greater force. I had to field a stream of inquiries from investors wanting to know what was going on. As we prepared to file for bankruptcy, there was only so much I could legally say publicly, even though outsiders could read some of the signs.

None of this was enjoyable by any stretch of the imagination, but I took some measure of quiet pride in doing as right by everyone as I could. I felt a bit like the captain going down with his ship.

I was hugely relieved when it was all finally behind me, but I knew that the experience had sharpened and tempered my business, management, and leadership abilities. I had learned that it's one thing to be principled when everything is going well; it's another to hold to those values when doing so is much more costly.

But as I contemplated the future, I wondered just how badly the Conxus failure would affect me.

Surprisingly, hardly at all, it seemed. Indeed, I even earned some favorable comments for the way I had handled the bankruptcy. I was surprised to receive a string of job offers as word of my availability got around. One of them even came from a Conxus investor who'd lost money in the collapse. He wanted me to consider becoming the CFO for one of his new interests.

"This wasn't your fault, Mark," he told me of the Conxus failure. "Of course, I'm disappointed at losing my money. But I was impressed with what you did through it all. I'd like you to work for me again." I did not end up accepting his offer, but I was grateful for his affirmation.

At first glance, Mike Wheeler and I make an unlikely pair: he a fair-haired white boy from the open plains of Iowa, reminiscent of Opie Taylor from *The Andy Griffith Show*, and I the black kid from the crowded streets of New York City.

But following the Conxus crash we quickly became good partners and great friends, on being twinned by a venture capital firm looking for leaders for their new technology start-up efforts. We worked together on a couple of projects that did not go very far, but we soon saw how well we fit: while our backgrounds might have been worlds apart, we shared many similarities and had complementary differences. We held matching values and offered varied strengths, his forward thinking and visionary and mine detailed and systems oriented.

Though we moved on in different directions, we kept in mind the connection we had enjoyed. Then, one day in 2002, Mike called.

"I think I have got something."

With service in the Marine Corps and success with a couple of start-ups in telecommunications under his belt before we met, Mike had an idea to bring those two worlds together through Internet protocol, or IP, services. Still in its infancy at that time, the technology brought telephone connection capabilities online, bypassing the need for all the hardware and physical infrastructure of traditional phone systems. The potential was huge.

A measure of the closeness and trust we already shared was that we detailed the terms of our working agreement on a napkin at the restaurant where we ate to talk through the details.

Mike saw a clever way of securing a foothold in this emerging market. He knew of a communications company that was looking to sell off a small services division that was losing money on an existing IP concern. The relatively minor operation was centered on providing service to Nigeria, where there were all kinds of problems getting payment from clients. Mike wanted to buy the business, pull out of the West Africa operation, and redirect the services to the military.

He was ahead of the curve in his thinking. Today, we are so used to living in a globally networked world, with virtually instant access to anyone, anywhere, simply by going online, that it's hard to picture a time when that wasn't so. But that was where things stood when we launched Segovia.

From his service background, Mike also knew that, despite its vast resources, the military had neither the equipment nor the personnel to develop its own global system. Rather than being one giant, seamless organization, the military was a collection of siloed interests, each often focused just on its own responsibilities and looked for outside contractors to provide many essential services.

Gradually, and gratefully, we were able to ease out of Nigeria and refocus the business. We presented Segovia at military trade shows, where our services were welcomed by those in uniform looking for solutions to communications headaches created by expanding overseas operations, post 9/11. We had struck a rich seam of need. Voice, video, data, whatever they needed access to, however remotely, we could deliver, connecting command centers in the United States instantly with teams in tents out in Iraq and Afghanistan. Importantly, too, we could encrypt their communication.

One of our first contracts was with the U.S. Army Space and

Missile Defense Command in Colorado Springs, Colorado. The U.S. Army Corps of Engineers was next. Combat Support Systems was another early user.

We started with a single earth station in Maryland but quickly built a global network to handle the growing business. Mike found an existing European earth station we could link with, and we also built our own in the Netherlands, on the California coast, and in Australia to forge a global communications chain.

Having a worldwide customer network brought extra demands. I'd never been shy about putting in the time needed to get the work done, nor had Mike. Not untypically, we would be the last ones to walk to our cars in the parking lot late in the evening. But it didn't end there. As Jimmy Buffett sang, it's always five o'clock somewhere—though in our case, not time for someone to knock off and have a beer, but time for them to make an urgent call to Segovia for help before they finished their working day.

We'd get calls at three and four a.m. our time from users having some kind of trouble with their connection and needing to get back up and running again ASAP. These were military operations that could not afford to be blacked out. One Sunday I answered my phone as Brenda and I were getting ready to leave for church with Jenée and Markus. It was a lieutenant colonel calling from somewhere in the region they designated as South West Asia—the military kept their locations vague—because his network was down.

"You should go ahead without me," I told Brenda, loosening my tie and sitting down. "This could take some time." It was just one example of how I was pretty tethered to Segovia—even when we went away on vacation I'd regularly check my emails.

Not that I begrudged it. As far as I was concerned, that kind of commitment just came with the territory. We needed a team

that would do whatever it took to keep our clients perfectly sat-
isfied, and we could not ask anything of them that we were not
prepared to do ourselves.

Besides, we were reaping tremendous rewards. Business was
exploding, launching us into financial realms I had previously
only ever dreamed of. I'd done very well in my years with USA
Mobile, but this was of a whole other magnitude. For example,
I'd traveled first-class before—even flying on the Concorde one
time, when I needed to be back stateside in a hurry, for an especially important meeting—but now Mike and I bought a part
share in our own jet, because it made all the travel we were having to do somewhat easier.

I didn't throw money around like crazy, but I certainly
indulged some of my tastes. My Lexus, to be replaced in turn by a
Mercedes and then a Bentley, made the old leaky Marquis seem a
lifetime ago. And I was able to enjoy dressing well. A personal tailor came to the house to show me different fabrics and measure
me for a perfectly fitted suit—one for every day of the month.

High-end didn't have to mean blingy, though; my conservative fashion sense was more sixties James Bond than con-
temporary rapper. I stipulated no vents for my jackets, as I felt
that offered a helpfully more streamlined outline for someone
my height, and also insisted that the pockets be sewn shut so
that the jackets fell more cleanly. The closest I came to a flash
of statement was with my French cuffs, set off by nice cuff links
that offered a little sparkle without being too gaudy—enough to
accentuate everything else without becoming the focal point.

Overall, I spent money in the same kind of way that I aimed
to work—aiming for the best without drawing undue attention
to myself. My parents' emphasis on self-restraint remained: I
didn't feel the need to say, in effect, "Look at me!"

At the office, I loved working with Mike, with whom I had an easy rapport. We'd quickly gone from good partners to even better friends. Meanwhile, at home, we'd fallen into a fairly comfortable rhythm. Brenda carried the bulk of the responsibility there, having long before set her nursing career aside to be the anchor and bedrock of the family while I went out to provide. We got family season tickets and then a suite for the Washington Redskins, alongside Mike, enjoying the games together as special family time. And despite the increasing busyness and our round-the-clock access for clients, I managed to find some extra time to spend with Markus, having recognized how his older sister had missed out in some ways by my not being there for some of her big events.

That just meant the long hours I still spent at work were even more intense. Yet with all the demands, I did not feel stressed. Healthwise, everything was fine. I had my weekly basketball workouts, two hours of nonstop hustle. I also played racquetball fairly regularly. If anything, rather than feeling under pressure, I was energized, like I was surfing the perfect wave. Things were good.

And then I woke up in the hospital, having lost a month of my life.

CHAPTER 7

"YOU ARE GOING TO GET BETTER"

The morning after Brenda had abruptly left me alone in the hospital, I woke to the realization that everything was still the same and yet everything had changed.

The various tubes running from my body were physical evidence of what I knew deep in my being, that I was still physically incapacitated. I could feel my weakness in my limbs as I tried to flex and move them. I didn't know whether I would ever walk again, but the uncertainty did not scare me. I had a deep sense of calm, a peace that everything was going to be okay, however things turned out, because God was with me.

This quiet awareness of His presence was new: the feeling that He was somewhere close at hand was different from the sincere but slightly distant belief I'd held previously. I had no doubt that this unlikely strong assurance had to be a gift from outside me, something supernatural, because it ran so contrary to my usual take-charge nature.

I wasn't admitting or accepting defeat; I was surrendering—and there is a world of difference between the two. While remembering Mom's words of encouragement and Coach Wooden's advice had prompted me to let go, to open my hands to whatever would come, at the same time they also offered me great hope. I knew that if God's plan was for me to recover, I would—no matter what the obstacles—if I cooperated with Him. As my own goal, and in my own strength, recovery was a towering, intimidating mountain. In God's plan, and with His help, it was no more than an anthill.

All these thoughts swirled around, but I felt that I needed to keep them to myself for the time being. I was still coming to terms with everything that had happened over the past month, and all that might be to come, and it didn't seem wise to give anyone reason to wonder whether the strokes had affected me mentally by suddenly talking about God. I knew that what I had experienced was real, but I could understand that others might be doubtful. Time would tell.

Now that I was awake and shaking off the lingering effects of the induced coma, it was time to start working on recovery. But I was to discover right away that this journey would not follow a straight line.

The plan was to move me from Reston Hospital to Mount Vernon Hospital, a facility that offered the kind of specialized stroke care I needed.

I was excited when the nurses came into my room to prepare me for the ambulance ride: it signaled progress, that things were moving. I tried to stay relaxed as they lifted me to transfer me onto a gurney, but suddenly there was excruciating pain in my stomach. I groaned. Bending over me, one of the nurses had caught her identification badge lanyard in my feeding tube, pulling it from where it was anchored in the port in my side. Pain flared in my stomach and fluid started to leak out around the port.

Flustered, the team set me back onto my bed to make sure everything was reconnected properly. Then they decided to postpone my transfer for a couple of days, to ensure that there were no residual problems from the accident. Frustrating and disappointing, it was a cautionary lesson about the sometimes stop-start nature of recovery.

Once I finally arrived at Mount Vernon, on June 14, 2007, I was surprised at how quickly we got to work, however. I imagined I might have a day or two to get used to my new situation, but the morning after my transfer, a young man in scrubs and sneakers arrived at my bedside.

He introduced himself as Sandip and told me he was a physical therapist, one of three therapists who would be working with me while I was at Mount Vernon. Their goal was to get me out of there as soon as possible—to help me get established well enough in my recovery that I could be discharged home, for the next stage in the journey.

Sandip was bright and cheerful as he began to show me how to use a walker. His warm personality was soothing as the enormity of what had happened to me hit me again: I simply couldn't get about without this piece of basic equipment. Not long ago, it seemed to me, I had been racing up and down the basketball court; now I could not even stand on my own.

Sandip talked me through the right way to use the walker: sit on the side of the bed, take a firm grip of the walker with both hands, and then ease yourself up. Make sure you are well balanced before moving. Then use your arms to move the frame forward a little, and walk yourself up to it. Repeat.

I followed Sandip's instructions carefully, smiling when he

told me, "Well done." I felt a rush of elation as I stood, unaided, for the first time in several weeks. Though this was a small thing, it was also significant progress, because it meant I no longer needed to be tethered to a catheter. I could get up and take myself to the bathroom.

"Treat the walker like a car when you come back to bed," Sandip told me. "Back up until you feel your backside against the bed. Once you feel that, sit down. Then you can lay back down and pull your legs over."

Having successfully completed the move, I was both encouraged and sobered—I knew that I simply could not manage without the walker. Though it made me feel feeble, in some ways, it was also a welcome tool.

The simple personal freedom of being able to go to the bathroom alone, the reclaiming of some personal dignity, was a real boost to my spirits. How much that can mean was underscored through the man I shared a room with.

An older gentleman, he'd recently had one of his legs amputated. He kept the curtain separating our two sides of the room closed most of the time, but from beyond I could hear the dialogue of the movie *The Shawshank Redemption,* which he watched repeatedly on a personal video player. It was annoying: by the time I left, I could recite great chunks of the script from memory.

Each night I'd hear water pouring onto the floor from behind the curtain, a sound that puzzled me until one time a nurse came in shortly afterward. Calling the man's name in frustration, she told him, "How many times must I tell you, if you need to go to the bathroom, ring the call bell!"

So that's what was going on. When I finally realized, it made me aware of how the strokes had slowed my thinking, such that I didn't work out what was happening, and grateful that I had been spared a similar indignity.

One night I was awakened by a sudden commotion on the other side of the room. "I need help, I need help," I heard a nurse calling. "Patient down!" Apparently the man on the other side of the curtain had tried to get himself to the bathroom unassisted and had fallen. Again, I was glad it hadn't been me.

There were still plenty of opportunities for me to learn to be humble. Having always been the guy in charge, it was difficult at times to admit that I needed help.

In addition to physical therapy, there was speech therapy and occupational therapy. Both are misnamed, in some ways. Speech therapy involves talking, but so much more. It's really about cognitive thinking, how we work through and learn to do things that become second nature. Tying your shoelaces, for example. I was stunned to find that, when asked, I did not remember how to tie my laces; I knew what needed to be done, what the end result looked liked, but simply could not visualize how to get there.

Occupational therapy is about more than what you do at work, too. It covers all the basic everyday tasks involved in taking care of yourself, like taking a shower. You may still know how to do that, but a stroke can affect your ability to complete the task because it impairs your balance and movements. Having only ever undressed in front of my wife, I found it a little uncomfortable to have to partially disrobe in front of Allison, a petite occupational therapist, so she could coach me through the process of taking a shower.

Even something as previously simple as brushing my teeth

turned out to require some extra concentration. You don't realize how important balance is to something as basic as using a
toothbrush, until it is compromised. I had to be sure I was well
placed in front of the sink so that my movements did not cause
me to wobble.

In the early days after the strokes, the use of my left side
was very limited. This made another everyday routine, applying
deodorant, a challenge. Another humbling part of my time in
the hospital was having to eat pureed food, like a baby, because
having the breathing tube in so long had left my throat tender.

Fortunately I had been spared one problem faced by some
people who have a stroke: losing some control of the muscles in
their throat, affecting their ability to swallow. While I was still
an inpatient at Mount Vernon, Vicky, my speech therapist, had
given me a Ritz cracker with peanut butter on it, and a glass
of water, and instructed me to eat and drink them—a "swallow test" to assess how well I could do so and determine when I
could graduate to real food again.

Forty-five-minute therapy sessions twice a day took it out of
me, so I spent a great deal of my free time sleeping, time when
my brain was busy healing.

Much as those early days were tough, there were moments
of unexpected humor, splashes of sunlight through the gray.
When Father's Day came around, soon after my arrival at Mount
Vernon, Mike turned up in my room.

"I've given Brenda the day off," he told me. "She's been with
you every night so far, and I think she needs a break. I'm gonna
spend the day with you." I was touched that my friend would sac-
rifice Father's Day with his family to care for mine.

We spent the day mostly quietly. We'd chat about sports and

work, then watch some television for a while. Mike would read a book while I dozed. When I got up to go to the bathroom, he was concerned. "Do you need help?"

"No, I've got it," I told him, confident I could manage on my own. Following Sandip's instructions, I one-stepped my way to the bathroom with my walker; I was making more trips than before the strokes because my bladder muscles had been weakened through nonuse during the weeks I had been catheterized. On the way back, I decided that I must surely have improved enough not to need to do that backing-in thing to get back into bed. So I just put the walker by the side of the bed and then turned.

The next thing I knew, I was lying facedown on the bed, unable to move. Without enough muscle control, I'd simply collapsed—thankfully not onto the floor like my roommate.

"Oh my God, are you okay?" Mike jumped up and lunged to help. "Brenda's going to kill me!"

"I'm okay," I told him, half-muffled by the pillow as he moved to right me. "It's my fault," I said. "They told me what to do; I just didn't do it the way they said."

Safely back in bed, I realized again that recovery was, in one way, out of my hands. I could help in it, but I could not hurry it along. It would take as long as it would take.

Order restored, Mike and I laughed together.

"Tell you what," I said to him. "You don't tell anyone about this; I won't tell anyone."

"Agreed!"

When I broke that pact some months later, I got a shock. During a conversation with Sandip, whom I happened to meet at a social event, I mentioned to him that I'd had a tumble when not using my walker properly on a trip to the bathroom.

He looked shocked. "When was this?"

"When I was in the hospital," I said, "Father's Day."

"You'd only just arrived then."

"Yeah," I agreed.

"Oh my goodness," he said. "When I showed you how to use the walker, don't you remember me telling you to use the call button to call a nurse?"

"No, why?"

"There's no way you're supposed to go to the bathroom on your own that soon," Sandip told me. "It's way too dangerous. Anything could have happened. You are supposed to make sure a nurse is there to help you."

Fortunately, my misunderstanding did not have any serious consequences, but it was just another example of how I would miss bits and pieces of information and instruction in the early days of my recovery as my brain tried to get back up to speed.

The incident spotlighted the importance of the two things that kept me going as I tried to find my way back to normal. There was the awareness that God was with me and that He would give me the strength for whatever I was facing. And there was Brenda's ever-constant presence and her loving care and encouragement.

She had been by my side almost constantly since arriving at Reston Hospital on the afternoon of May 12, other than for the evening she left me alone after I woke up and the Father's Day break Mike insisted she needed. She'd slept either in a chair at the side of my bed or in one of the chairs out in the intensive care unit waiting room. Staff had let her use a vacant room from time to time to shower.

She'd raced home briefly occasionally to check on Jenée and Markus but always hurried back to be there should I wake. And once I was awake, she was there for me, every faltering step of the way.

We celebrated quietly together when, after two weeks at Mount Vernon, I was discharged on June 29, 2007. But arriving back home, with Brenda helping me from the car to the house in a wheelchair, we were reminded of the distance still to go. Once inside, I had to learn to navigate the stairs—going up and down on my backside, like an overgrown toddler, as I could not risk a fall if I were to stand.

It was good to be back home, to be with Jenée and Markus again, and to sit on my own sofa. But I knew that this was only the latest stage in my journey. After a weekend break, catching up on the phone with family glad to hear that I was out of the hospital, it was time to head back to Mount Vernon to begin my outpatient recovery in what they called the Bridge Program, for those who had suffered a traumatic brain injury.

I was a little subdued as Brenda helped me back into the car that Monday morning. Turning the engine on, she flipped the satellite radio from the jazz station we usually listened to over to an unfamiliar gospel channel. As we drove, my thoughts wandering to what lay ahead, the music seeped through my distraction like sunshine warming its way through clouds.

"Isn't that Jonathan Butler?" I asked. I thought I recognized the distinct voice and guitar work of the artist we knew as a smooth jazz star. Brenda and I had several of his CDs, and he'd autographed one for us when we had met him after seeing him play at a small club in Washington, DC.

I leaned forward and hit the info button on the dashboard.

Sure enough, Jonathan Butler was singing a song called "Lord I Lift Your Name on High" on Sirius's gospel channel:

> Lord I lift Your name on high
> Lord I love to sing Your praises
> I'm so glad You're in my life
> I'm so glad You came to save us
>
> You came from heaven to earth
> To show the way
> From the earth to the cross
> My debt to pay
> From the cross to the grave
> From the grave to the sky
> Lord I lift Your name on high

Brenda and I smiled at each other as the words washed over us. I felt like this was a message from God, reminding me that He had come to me and that He would show me the way: all I had to do was keep trusting Him and looking to Him for help. I thought of all that Jesus had gone through, the betrayal and crucifixion, so that I could have a relationship with God the Father. What I faced was nothing in comparison.

God, please just give me the strength for whatever You send my way.

I would soon need that reminder, because my newfound faith was challenged hard on that first day back at Mount Vernon as an outpatient. I arrived in a wheelchair and went through a battery of evaluations designed to gauge my limitations and assess what needed to be worked on to help me get back as far as possible to life before the strokes.

In one session, I was given a wooden clothespin and asked, "Can you open this?"

I thought, *Duh, of course,* but answered, "Sure."

"Why don't you open it with your left hand," Lisa said, passing it to me. I took the clothespin but could not open it. No matter how much I concentrated, my fingers would not do what I willed them to.

Next, she gave me seven words she said she wanted me to remember, like *window, door, ceiling.* Then she asked me some questions about where I had gone to school, what I had studied, and my work. After several minutes' conversation, she paused.

"Okay, I want to come back to those words I gave you a few minutes ago," Lisa said. "Do you remember?"

My mind was completely blank. I could not remember a single word.

Lisa must have seen the crestfallen look on my face. "Don't worry, Mark," she said. "You have suffered a brain injury and some of your brain cells have been scarred. They have to be retrained to do these things, and we are going to help you."

That was encouraging, but there would be more reminders of the scale of the task ahead of me. When Lisa placed a checkbook in front of me, describing a scenario in which I had to pay someone for their work, and asked me to write the check, I could only stare at the paperwork in front of me, frozen, until she gently guided me through, step by step.

"You are going to get better," Lisa assured me.

As if I needed further encouragement, when Brenda and I got back into the car at the end of the day to go home, that same Jonathan Butler song came on the radio: "Lord I Lift Your Name on High." It would play each time we made the trip to and from Mount Vernon over the next few days.

It was just as well, as there were to be more reminders of the severity of my strokes. In another assessment, I was asked to read a sports article online. When I tried to comply, I was horrified; it made no sense whatsoever. It read as a jumble of incomplete thoughts and sentences. My heart sank; maybe I was worse than I had believed.

My occupational therapist, Gloria, then sat me in front of a board with rows of lights that flashed on and off randomly and had me hit them when they lit up. It seemed like a dumb children's game to me, but I complied and hit every light—or so I thought. But when I finished, Gloria told me that I had missed a bunch of them. My initial reaction was further disappointment, but it turned out to be potential good news. The poor results suggested that some of the outer part of my field of vision seemed to have been affected, Gloria said—not an uncommon consequence of a stroke—and I needed to go see an ophthalmologist.

There I underwent a series of further tests and exams and was told that I had lost around ninety percent of the peripheral vision on my left-hand side. The news prompted mixed feelings. I was disappointed to learn that the stroke had affected my vision so much, but I was greatly relieved that it explained my failure to understand what I had been reading. I hadn't lost my mind, just my ability to see to the corner of the page.

With a clearer picture of where I was and where I wanted to be, my therapists tailored a recovery program for me. Three times a week Brenda and I would make the drive to Mount Vernon, where I would have physical, occupational, and speech therapy.

Some people assume that physical and occupational therapy must be the hardest, because you are practicing physical actions and movements over and over. They certainly are physically demanding, and I would be drained by the time I had finished the sessions, but I found speech therapy the toughest.

While PT and OT took it out of me, they were at least something I could see and feel. I knew I was making progress by the way I performed; I could sense the repetitive actions becoming second nature again, and I could see my strength and range of motion improving. Speech therapy, on the other hand, was more conceptual. Focused on retraining the cognitive processes in my brain, progress seemed less concrete. And because my therapists were intent on helping me recover so that I could function at the demanding level I had before my strokes, they pushed me hard.

All of it was tiring work, but I kept at it. I told the therapists not to let up on me; I'd do everything they asked. I dug deep into the reserves of determination and doggedness that had always helped me previously. But there was a difference. I didn't apply myself with the quiet pride I used to have, but with a new measure of humility, knowing that while I could do everything within my power, some things were ultimately only in God's power to change.

The day-to-day reality of my situation helped keep me humble. I wasn't involved in a booming business, managing big money. I was stacking and restacking piles of dishes in the rehabilitation department's faux kitchen, where we patients practiced everyday domestic chores to retrain our brains and strengthen limbs weakened by stroke.

Back home, I applied myself to the homework we were given, basic exercises like putting a towel on the floor beneath my bare feet and using my toes to scrunch it up. These simple, repetitive routines helped me relearn fine motor skills and reprogram my brain.

While I was learning to let go and trust God, I was at the same time determined to make sure I did my part. I knew that though He was in charge, that didn't mean I just got to sit back and wait. I was willing to accept whatever God had for me, but I didn't want to miss out on anything because of my own lack of effort.

That positive focus led me to decide not to install a hand bar in our shower. Washing was still tricky, especially when I needed to balance on one leg. But I felt that relying on an aide too soon might keep me from improving as much as possible. If it turned out I really needed one, we could always add it later. For the time being, I was prepared to just go slow and wobble a bit, determined somehow not to fall over.

Through it all, Brenda was my chauffeur, champion, coach, and cheerleader. She drove me to all my outpatient therapy appointments at Mount Vernon, about an hour from home. She handled all the health insurance details and made sure I got all the treatment and care that was available. She sat in on every therapy session I had, never interrupting or commenting, just a quiet, encouraging presence at the back of the room. If I'd forget something I had been told or learned at the hospital when I was later doing therapy exercises on my own at home, she would gently remind me. She'd help me practically, but only when I just couldn't do something for myself, like tying my own shoelaces in the early days, before my fine motor skills improved.

And, perhaps most important, she kept telling me that she believed in me, that I was going to make it, and that she was with me all the way.

CHAPTER 8

"YOU'VE GOT TO TRUST HIM"

My recovery program was like going back to school in more ways than one. I had to relearn things I'd known since childhood, such as tying my shoelaces. Repeating these exercises helped regroove my brain, so that over time they once more became second nature, rather than something I had to concentrate on.

Because my head felt a little fuzzy in the early days, I found it helped to use word and picture association to remember people's names, among other things. I also took notes to remind me of what I needed to do, and I developed the habit of reading things twice to be sure I understood, and highlighting what was really important.

At the Bridge I was encouraged to use my iPad to play word-search games; the therapists said this helped retrain my brain, rather than letting it settle in its slightly jumbled state. I'd never been much for word puzzles before, but I diligently spent ten to fifteen minutes a day working on them. Trying to beat my previous time drove me to work hard, and succeeding was an encouraging sign of progress.

As well as working my muscle memory, I also had to work my muscles. My left side was notably weaker than my right, but I deliberately focused on using my left arm and hand to do things, rather than defaulting to my stronger right side. As a consequence, I learned not to fill a glass of water or a cup of coffee too full, because otherwise my weaker left hand would shake a little and cause a spill.

But not everything was going to return to the way it was. I also had to learn how to adapt to some of the physical limitations resulting from my strokes, like my reduced vision. That involved remembering to turn my head regularly to scan my "blacked-out" left side to see what was there. Even so, there would still be—and still are—times when someone who did not know about my limited peripheral vision would approach me on that side and think I was ignoring them, unaware that I didn't see them out of the corner of my eye.

Thankfully my speech had not been seriously affected. I had to think carefully about some words, to begin with, and Lisa helped me work on regaining some of the intonation I'd lost, a common result of a stroke that left me sounding a little flat when I talked.

Just as I tried to be a diligent student in recovery, I also realized that I had much more to learn about God and His ways.

One of the first discoveries I made as I became aware of His constant presence, not limited merely to Sunday mornings at church, was that surrendering to Him was not a one-and-done act. I'd meant it from the bottom of my heart when I'd lain in the hospital that night and told Him I was okay with whatever He brought my way.

But as a type A person used to getting things done, I learned that letting go of the reins was only step one. Not trying to take them back when life was not going my way or as quickly as I thought it should was step two—and three and four and more. I came to realize that I needed to repeat that surrender every day, especially when setbacks and frustrations came along.

It was helpful to remember that, irked as I was that I couldn't just apply my old work-harder approach to move things along faster, I was in far better shape than some of the others at the Bridge. I was having to recover and relearn some things, but I had not completely lost any major functions or abilities, as some others had.

Part of letting go meant swallowing my pride. I'd never been one to grandstand and make a show of myself, but it had been important for me to be seen by others as someone who had it all together, who was in control and typically in charge. Clearly this was no longer the case, with me shuffling around at first with a walker, and later a cane.

My frailties seemed to be exposed even more in some of the group rehab sessions that brought patients together from our individualized recovery tracks, which were tailored to our differing needs and circumstances. Our roots were different— strokes and accidents—but the fruit we were dealing with was the same: a traumatic brain injury.

A bunch of us would be taken out to the mall, to a restaurant, to a bowling alley, and to ride the train. These trips were intended to expose us to some of the everyday challenges of being out and about in public in a safe setting, and to provide opportunities for developing our motor skills: bowling was a great way of working on balance and coordination.

I threw myself into these activities, though I always thought we must have stuck out like a sore thumb to passersby wondering what was wrong with us. Sometimes being in a group was more discouraging than embarrassing. During one early outpatient session at the hospital, we were presented with a workplace scenario: a postal worker was trying to print a letter from his computer but could not make it happen. Why?

The answer seemed fairly obvious, I thought, grumbling to myself about this worthless exercise. "Well, I'd guess that the printer is broken," I suggested to Amalya, the stand-in speech therapist who was covering for Lisa that day.

"Oh no," said a woman in the group. "I worked at the post office for years, so I know what the problem is. His boss won't listen to him. I went through that kind of stuff for years."

My heart sank as she spoke. *How could I have missed all that?* My brain must really have been fried not to have seen that. I went home really down.

But the next day, Amalya took me to the side. "Sorry about yesterday, Mark," she said. "You were right about the printer problem. You're in the wrong class; we'll get you out of there and into a different group."

Relief that I had been right was quickly followed by irritation at what seemed to me to be the simplicity of the exercise, an annoyance that must have registered on my face. "Every patient is different, Mark, and we try to tailor things to their needs," she said, "but it can take time to evaluate exactly where people are and what they need." I realized that I needed to be more patient—with myself and with others.

To be fair, the staff was mostly fantastic. They were always encouraging and affirming, knowing when to push patients to try that little bit harder and when to back off and be sympathetic. This supportive environment extended to even the non-therapeutic staff.

Alan, part of the administrative team, always seemed to have an eye for when I was having a tough day. "Hey," he would say cheerily, "don't focus on today. Today may be a bad day; don't worry about it. Tomorrow will be a whole 'nother day, and everything is going to be entirely different." He was right, but sometimes I would still lose sight of the big picture because I got caught up in all the frustrating little details.

Such had been the case about a month into my outpatient rehab time when Brenda and I got into the car to head home after a day of working on my recovery. I was tired and frustrated. I didn't feel like I was making enough progress, so I reverted to my old ways and tried to work out how to fix the problem.

The issue, I decided, was the therapists: they just weren't the right fit, the best people to help me.

"Bren, it's just not working with them," I said. "You're going to have to talk to someone in the office there and get me new therapists. They're just not good enough."

Brenda pushed back gently. "Now, Tony, they're just fine. What's the problem?"

I vented some more. "No, Bren, they're terrible," I said, listing all the ways they didn't get me and weren't what I needed. "They have to go."

Brenda didn't answer. Instead, she pulled over to the side of the Fairfax County Parkway and brought the car to a halt. We sat quietly for a moment as the commuter traffic flashed by, and then she turned to me.

"Tony," she said, with the tone that told me I should listen up good, not unkind but firm. "You have no idea what the good

Lord has in store for you. How do you know that He didn't allow you to have these strokes because He wants you to show other people that you can recover from them? You've got to trust Him. I know it's hard, but you've just got to trust Him in all this, okay?"

There was a moment of stillness, and then she checked her mirror and pulled back out into the traffic. We didn't speak much more the rest of the way back to the house, but I mulled over what she'd said. *You know,* I thought, *Brenda's right. Maybe God is using me. Maybe I'm going to get to show others that you can come back from something like this, that there's still hope.*

As I thought about it, I realized that the therapists weren't really the problem; I was just directing my frustration at them because the nature of their work with me meant that they were more often exposing the areas where I still needed to progress. In fact, I recognized, I'd also grumbled a bit—to myself, at least—about my inpatient therapist at Mount Vernon.

So I took Brenda's admonishment to heart, redoubling my efforts: if God did have a plan in it all, I didn't want to mess things up by not doing my part.

One of the first things I had done upon getting home from the hospital was to dig out a Bible, usually only picked up to take to church on Sundays. I wasn't much of a student of the Scriptures, but I knew Mom's *God only gives you what He knows you can handle* encouragement was in there somewhere. I found it in the New Testament, in 1 Corinthians 10:13:

"No temptation has overtaken you that is not common to man. God is faithful, and he will not let you be tempted beyond your ability, but with the temptation he will also provide the way of escape, that you may be able to endure it."

What struck me as I read the verse was that while God promised a way out, He didn't say He would pick me up and carry me to the exit. He just said that He would provide one; I had to make my own way there.

At the same time, I was aware that enthusiasm and determination can take you only so far: sometimes you have to just let things take their time. For example, I came to realize, while I had to be diligent in doing all my physical exercises, pushing too hard could be counterproductive, simply overtiring me. I had to pace myself. Here was another area in which I had a lot to learn—discerning where to press on and where to let go.

That required recognizing that while some things may be possible, they may not be wise. One concern I had as I worked on my recovery was whether I would be able to play basketball again. I loved the exercise, the camaraderie, and the challenge: no one out on the court cared about your job or how much money you made. They just wanted to know whether you would give it your all. I missed those Thursday night games down at the high school.

The doctors told me that there should be no problem with my playing hoops again. They had left a hole in the back of my skull where they had drilled it open to save my life, but they were confident that the muscle there would thicken and provide enough protection for my brain. Still, as I thought about the potential risk, and how a degree of caution would keep me from really giving it my all when I was playing, I decided that my hoop days were over, as were my racquetball sessions, for the same reason. I didn't want to go out there if I was putting myself—and my family, as a result—at unnecessary risk, and if I couldn't play with one hundred percent of my effort.

I lamented this decision to my old school friend Lenny when he came to visit. He was still back in Queens, working as a plumber. Though our paths had diverged over the years, we had kept in touch on and off. He'd been in my wedding party, and I would be his best man in due course. When I got home from the hospital after my strokes, he came out to stay to see how I was doing.

I told him that I knew it was best not to play basketball again, but I was disappointed.

"Sounds like you need the Serenity Prayer," he told me.

"What's that?" I asked.

"God, grant me the serenity to accept the things I cannot change, the courage to change the things I can, and the wisdom to know the difference," he recited.

The words rang a bell as he spoke them, though I remembered them as something usually quoted by people in recovery from one kind of addiction or another. But as I chewed on them, I realized they were true for my situation too.

Once more, I reflected on how surrendering to God meant unlearning some of my old ways of doing things, confident that I knew best, and learning to look and listen for His quiet leading and direction.

On August 31, 2007, after two months of regular visits to Mount Vernon, I was told I was ready to "graduate." I'd progressed enough that I could continue pursuing recovery on my own. What would I do next Monday, instead of coming for rehab, I was asked by Sharon, one of the Bridge team, in my exit interview.

"Well, I guess I'll go in to the office," I said. "You know, back to work."

She looked a little surprised. "Really, Mark?"

"Yes, why not?"

"Well, most people don't go back to work right away. They give it a bit of time."

"Oh," I said. "How long?"

"Some people wait up to a year."

A year? I couldn't believe it. Sitting around at home and watching some of the daytime television shows I had never seen before had been fun for a short time, after I got back from the hospital, but I couldn't imagine doing that for months to come. "So, what do they do?"

"They are still recovering in different ways..."

"If I need to do some more work here at rehab, then I'll keep coming back," I told her. "If I'm finished because the insurance has run out, then I'll pay for whatever else I need to do myself. But if I'm done here, then I am going to go back to work."

Sharon tried to press me to reconsider, to agree to take things easy a bit longer, but I was adamant. I met with the supervisor of the program to express my concern and tell her what I was thinking. The supervisor listened and agreed with me.

"There's nothing more we can do here that you can't do on your own," she said. "I think you are okay to go back to work. But do me one thing, will you? Make it part-time to start with."

That seemed reasonable enough, and I knew that I wasn't going to return to my twelve-hour-day routine anyway, for a couple of reasons. One was physical; though I had recovered remarkably, I knew it was not wise to push myself too hard. The other was the inner changes still going on. Having been given a second lease on life, I wanted to focus more of it on my new-found deeper faith and my relationships.

I had been very touched to learn how much care and concern people had expressed to Brenda and others in our family during the crisis days of my strokes. She told me how Mike and Teresa and others had been pillars of support to her during the most desperate hours, when she did not know how badly the strokes had affected me.

I also pieced together parts of the story myself, as fragments of memory from my time in intensive care came to the surface. I could recall snatches of interaction with visitors, including Mike. His father-in-law, Dick Lynch, who was retired military, had also regularly come to sit by my bed and keep me company.

There were also lots of get-well messages from staff at Segovia. Mike kept me abreast of what was happening there, even asking my opinion on some business decisions that needed to be made, which I appreciated. It made me feel that he hadn't just plowed ahead without me. The company had grown to about 125 employees by this stage, but though business was booming, we still had much of a small-company feel. People knew one another and got along well.

So when, a few weeks into my outpatient rehab program, Mike suggested I drop by the office—it was on the way from the hospital to home—and say hello to everyone, I didn't think twice. I was wearing my rehab workout gear—loose pants, T-shirt, and sneakers, a far cry from my usual sharp business attire—and still using my walker to get about when we made the visit. I was quite gaunt, too, but somehow I wasn't bothered that people weren't going to see the Mark Moore they had known. This was the new one; the same in many ways, but also a bit humbled, and more appreciative.

Many of the staff came out to the reception area to greet me. My eyes filled with tears as I saw their smiles, and my voice cracked as I thanked them for their cards, their messages of support and encouragement, and their prayers. I told them that

I was grateful to them, and to God, and that with His help I would be back at some stage.

I stayed for only a few minutes, because I was tired after a busy day at rehab, but it was great to see everyone. After my few words to them all, I got to visit with some of them one-on-one and enjoy some lighthearted moments.

As we drove home later, Brenda said, "Now I know you're coming back, Mark."

"What do you mean?"

"Your laugh," she said of the chuckle that I was well-known for among family and friends. "I heard your laugh today for the first time since you were in the hospital."

CHAPTER 9

"A DIFFERENT WORLD"

Lenny's encouraging visit toward the end of my outpatient time didn't only help me put things in perspective; it gave me a new goal to focus on.

When I told him that I had reluctantly decided to hang up my sports shoes, he asked, "Have you ever thought of running instead?"

I hadn't. I'd been pretty fast when I was a kid, but I'd never been that interested in running just for running's sake. Driving toward the net, hustling on the racquetball court, or racing to the next base provided a reason for all that effort, it seemed to me.

An avid runner himself, having completed the famous New York City and Boston Marathons, Lenny urged me to consider taking up running. "It could replace your loss of basketball," he said.

I knew that I needed something to fill the gap left by basketball and racquetball, because not playing them had taken its toll. The morning of my first part day back at work, I'd relished the prospect of dressing sharply again—very different attire from my recovery wardrobe. Fresh from the shower, I selected a dress shirt and was surprised when I could not get the top collar buttons closed at my neck. *Oh well,* I thought, *maybe the dry cleaner used too much starch.* I just cinched my tie up tight to disguise the open collar.

But when I pulled my jacket on, it felt taut across my shoulders and did not sit well at the front.

"Bren," I called, "I think something's going on with the dry cleaners. They must be shrinking my clothes somehow."

Brenda came and stood close, by my walk-in closet.

"Actually, sweetie," she said gently, "you've put on a little bit of weight, you know."

Surprised, I went to the bathroom scale. Sure enough, she was right. I weighed around 185 pounds, well over the usual 160 I had maintained most of my adult life. I was shocked. The last time I had checked my weight had been before I was discharged from the hospital, when, looking a little frail after going six weeks or so without solid food, I had tipped the scales at just 150 pounds. That meant I had packed on around 35 pounds in just two months.

Looking back over my rehabilitation, I realized that while I had been physically active, it was at nowhere near the intensity or rate of my previous pattern of exercise. Plus, once I was home from the hospital and able to eat solid food again, I had indulged myself a little. Whenever Mike called to ask if he could drop by and whether I wanted him to bring anything, I always requested a large Robeks smoothie, one of my favorite treats. I figured because I chose a fruity one it must be healthy. I'd also allowed myself more chocolates and soda than I usually consumed, as a bit of a reward for my rehab efforts.

As I looked at myself in the mirror, squeezed too tightly into one of my favorite suits, I knew it was time for some drastic action. Though I was determined to get my weight down again, I realized it would take some time, so I bought three larger suits for the time being. Then I signed up for a weight-loss meal program. It was awful, like eating cobwebs; I half thought of throwing the contents away and eating the packaging instead. I gave up after two days, keeping the breakfast servings—because, after all, you have to work pretty hard to mess up a simple breakfast—and tossing the remaining twenty-eight days of lunch and dinner servings.

Instead, I decided to take more control of my own choices. Out went the chocolate, the Robeks, and the sodas. I switched from whole milk to skim milk. What made the biggest difference, however, was when I picked up on Lenny's suggestion and put on a pair of running shoes.

Having done quite a lot of walking on a treadmill as part of my rehabilitation, I figured it might help if I picked up the pace—and that having a goal would spur me on. I decided that I was going to run a 5k as close to the first anniversary of my strokes as possible.

The therapists at Mount Vernon were cautiously encouraging. Always looking to harness a patient's enthusiasm whenever they could, they gave me some advice on how to carefully up my workouts. I had started walking with the treadmill setting at one and a half miles per hour—a more-than-leisurely forty-minute-mile pace, which nevertheless left me feeling winded at first. Gradually, over time, I increased the speed. I used the treadmill at Mount Vernon and then at home and began visiting our health club a couple of times a week to walk around the indoor track there.

I knew that I must have looked pretty pathetic to anyone else working out, but I just tuned that awareness out. Instead, I plugged into my iPod, on which I had loaded all my favorite newly discovered gospel tunes. The playlist would run for an hour or so, and I would plod away, stride after stride, until I had sweated my way through all the tunes. The songs helped me focus in on God rather than my circumstances, lifting my spirits and driving me on. Bit by bit I increased my speed.

I didn't tell anyone but Brenda and my therapists about my 5k plan, to start with. I just kept at it through the winter months. I found a 5k that would be a great fit: runners in the Race for Hope in Washington, DC, on Saturday, May 4, 2008, would be helping raise money for brain tumor research. Having signed up, I began to tell others about my goal. Several people said that they wanted to run with me, including one of our employees at Segovia. He asked me about my training and whether I had been running outside at all.

I told him no, it had all been on the treadmill, and he said that I needed to add some outdoor running to my preparation as soon as possible.

"Running outside is a whole different thing to running on a treadmill," he explained. "The treadmill sets your pace for you, so you don't have to think about it; you have to be able to pace yourself when you are running on your own. And being outside is a totally different environment. You've got hills and cracks in the sidewalk, and then there's the wind and the heat and all the changes in the weather. It's a different world outdoors, Mark."

What he said made sense. I measured just over a mile and a half from the house; there and back would make the 5k. First time out, I thought I was going to die. Without the treadmill setting to pace me, I set off way too fast and was soon gasping.

I ended up having to walk home, tail between my legs. But I decided that I would view this as a helpful learning experience rather than a setback. Next time out, I set off more cautiously.

Over time I got better at pacing myself, eventually clocking forty-two minutes for the route. I began to feel better, too, shedding those additional pounds and gaining a renewed sense of vitality. As I looked back, I realized that I'd probably been suffering a little bit of depression in those early days of recovery: the comfort-food diet on top of the natural weariness caused by all the therapy had left me feeling sluggish.

The outdoor training paid dividends. I was pumped when May 4 finally came around, setting out for Washington, DC, on a bus with about fifty family, friends, and supporters, all wearing matching light blue baseball caps. Brenda and Jenée had designed them: a bridge graphic and the words *Moore's Bridge Builders: Race for Hope, Washington DC, May 4, 2008*. About a dozen of the group were going to run with me—among them Lenny, who had come in from New York, Jenée and Markus, and some of the therapists from Mount Vernon, including Stephanie and Lisa. Vivian, the clinical coordinator at the Bridge, was pregnant, so she couldn't run, but she came and walked the course.

Sitting on the bus on the ride down, I offered a quiet prayer. I didn't ask God to help me break any records, just that He would give me the strength to finish and finish well. It was exciting to be part of such a large group of runners on a beautiful day, but I managed to avoid the temptation to run off too fast once we got started. Wearing my race number, 6375, I paced myself carefully—so well that before too long, it seemed, the leaders of the pack were coming back the other way on the out-and-back loop, heading to the finish. But these were elite runners, and I was not discouraged as I kept up my steady pace.

Lenny and Markus ran with me for the first stretch, but I could sense that I was holding them back. I told them to go on and I'd see them at the finish line. Imagine my delight when sometime later they each reappeared at my side, having completed their own races and then come back to find me and cross the line with me.

I finished to cheers, feeling strong; in fact, I felt like I could have run another mile or two, had I needed to. Looking over at the clock, I was amazed to realize that I had completed the race—my first ever—in just over thirty-six minutes, six minutes faster than I had ever managed to complete one of my training runs. Not bad for a middle-aged guy who couldn't walk properly a few months previously, and who a year before had nearly died.

Runner 6375 may have placed 683rd out of the 857 men running in the Race for Hope, but he felt like he had won gold.

Recovery doesn't happen without its share of setbacks, however. And I discovered that learning to trust God is an ongoing lesson, too, soon having an opportunity to test the depth of how far down and truly rooted was my belief that God was in control.

One area where it had been hard to let go was wanting to know what had caused the strokes. I still found it difficult to accept that the doctors couldn't tell me definitively why they had occurred. Brenda tried to assure me from her nursing background that it was not uncommon for some problems to have no clear cause; that was just the way things were in medicine. But from my numbers way of looking at the world, where everything could be accounted for, it didn't make a lot of sense.

If they didn't know what had caused the strokes, I reasoned, how could they be sure that I wouldn't have another one for the same reason? At my regular checkups, the doctors all assured me that I was in great health and that there was no reason to suspect a recurrence. So I tried my best to let go of my frustration over the uncertainty.

As the summer of 2008 rolled around, we made plans for a special trip to New York City. Markus had been a huge New York Mets fan ever since he was a kid, inheriting his father's and grandfather's genes, but had never gotten to see an actual game at the famed Shea Stadium. His spectating had been limited to the television. With Shea scheduled for demolition the following year, we arranged a special weekend trip so that Markus could experience his team on their historic diamond. I got tickets for all four of us, and also arranged for Lenny and his son, Dakari, and daughter, Sharice, to join us.

The day before the game, a Friday, I was at work when I was suddenly struck with tremendous back pain, deep and throbbing. I knew I hadn't pulled or twisted anything, but I could hardly move. The pain didn't pass as the afternoon wore on, so I took myself to the ER at the nearby hospital. There they checked me over and couldn't find anything wrong. Probably just back strain, someone suggested, prescribing some painkillers to take the edge off. If I took it easy I should be fine again by Monday, the doctor told me.

The medication helped to a degree, but I was still in considerable discomfort when we set out on Saturday for New York. Brenda knew I was in pain, but I was trying to play it low-key because I was determined that Markus was going to get to see his game. We didn't mention anything to him or Jenée, but they could tell from the time it took me to walk from the parking lot to the stadium and then climb the steps to our seats that something was up.

Afterward I told Brenda I had to get some help. We said

good-bye to Lenny, Dakari, and Sharice and settled Jenée and Markus in the hotel we were booked into, and then the two of us went to a nearby ER. I told them about going to the ER back in Virginia and about the painkillers I'd been prescribed. They ran some tests but couldn't find anything wrong, either. They gave me some more meds and sent us on our way.

I got through the night but was still in so much pain the next morning that I went back to the ER. They looked me over again but said they could not see anything wrong. They told me to go home and follow up with my doctor if I still needed to.

The trip home was agony. There was a traffic accident somewhere up ahead, which slowed us down, and being stuck in the car for an extended period somehow made the pain even worse. I simply could not get comfortable. Grateful to finally make it back to the house, I crawled upstairs and went to bed, having taken enough painkillers to get me through an unsettled night.

The next morning, my back still hurt, but I found when I tried to get out of bed that my left leg was also grotesquely swollen. Brenda took one look and said, "Honey, you need to get to a doctor right away." With great relief I managed to get an early appointment with my family doctor. John Phillips checked me over, noting how badly swollen my leg had become, and asked about my strokes the previous year. Hadn't there been a blood clot issue? he wanted to know.

His question needled my frustration about not knowing exactly what had happened and why. "They said I'd gotten blood clots, but they didn't know whether the stroke caused the clots or the other way round," I told him.

"Well, I think I can answer your question now," he said. "I think that a blood clot was the cause. I think you've got a blood clot now, and that's what is causing your leg to swell." He told me

I needed to go straight over to a nearby clinic for a sonogram. There a technician spread gel on my stomach and leg to allow a transducer to glide over my skin for a Doppler ultrasound. Having scanned me, he told me to wait while he went and consulted with Dr. Phillips.

He was away for what seemed to be a long time. My mind started to wander as I waited. I didn't worry that I might have blood clots or be in danger of another stroke. No, I went to darker places. *I hope it isn't cancer,* I thought, recalling how it had taken Mom and Michael, who had succumbed to stomach cancer in 1989, aged thirty-eight.

I tried to read the tech's face when he came back into the room. Impassive, he reached for the phone, dialed a number, and then passed me the handset. "Your doctor wants to speak with you."

That really scared me; it must be serious if Dr. Phillips had to do the talking. I guessed he wouldn't tell me over the phone that it was cancer but that he would ask me to go and see him so he could break the news in person. I tried to brace myself as I took the phone.

"Mark," he said, "you do have blood clots, as I suspected. That's what has been causing the pain." For a moment I was relieved, not hearing the word *cancer,* but he went on. "We need to get this cleared up right away. Here's what I want you to do: I want you to go straight to Fairfax Hospital. Don't go home. Go right there, okay? I'm going to call them now to have you admitted."

Though I was glad that my worst fears had not been realized, his tone and urgency were unsettling. I reminded myself of my encounter that last time I'd been admitted to the hospital: *God only gives you what He knows you can handle.*

Things slowed down a bit at Fairfax Hospital, which made me

feel a bit better; the less the urgency, the smaller the problem, I figured. They ran some further tests and kept me overnight.

"It's a deep vein thrombosis, or DVT," the doctor told me the next morning. I'd developed a blood clot in my deep leg vein, he explained. Blood that should have been flowing freely was backed up as a result, causing the pain. Untreated, the condition could cause permanent damage to my leg—or even kill me.

Though clots often break down gradually over time, to be absorbed by the body, they can break away and flow up into the body, getting trapped in the lungs. Here they can block the oxygen supply, causing heart failure: a pulmonary embolism.

Just such an incident had recently claimed the life of NBC *Meet the Press* moderator Tim Russert, I vaguely recalled. There had been some discussion about whether his incident had been precipitated by a long flight he had recently taken, as sitting in a confined situation for an extended period—as I'd experienced in our snail's pace drive back from New York—can increase the likelihood of clots forming.

Clots can also travel to the brain and cause a stroke— something I definitely did not want to face the prospect of again.

"We want to perform a catheter-directed thrombolysis," the doctor told me, explaining that would involve inserting a thin wire into a vein to break up the clot. "You should be fine, but we do need to do this right away." Laid facedown, I was given a local anesthetic for the procedure and tried to remain still as the wire was pushed into the vein behind my knee. With that completed, I was prescribed Coumadin, a blood thinner, to ensure there would be no more clots in the future. With the immediate danger passed, I was then referred to a hematologist to see whether he might be able to determine more about the blood deficiency that had caused the DVT.

That would involve switching me from Coumadin to another anticoagulant, Lovenox, for a period—for reasons I did not fully understand—so that further tests could be carried out. Then it would be possible to identify the exact form of my blood deficiency. However, I would still have to go back onto Coumadin for the rest of my life.

Now that I finally had the opportunity to get to the bottom of what had been going on, I decided it wasn't worth the time, money, and upset to my regimen to find out. After all, I'd still be on the same medication afterward. Instead, I just decided to have Jenée and Markus tested, to ensure that they had not inherited the same deficiency, putting them at risk too.

When their results came back negative, I decided to just let go of the need to know. I thought about it and concluded that while I might not know the exact whys and wherefores of my health crisis, I did know for sure that God had allowed it, for some reason I did not and may never know. Neither of my parents had been diagnosed with a blood deficiency, nor my siblings, nor my children; was it really just a random chance that I had one? I didn't think so.

"I just believe that this is the way He wanted me to be," I told Brenda, remembering her words that time when she had pulled over to the side of the road as we drove home from a rehab session. "We don't know what the good Lord might have in store: maybe He has something He wants us to do."

CHAPTER 10

"YOU HAVE TO GET NAKED"

As an accountant, I know that every small detail matters. Get one wrong, and things just won't add up properly. I believe that what's true on a spreadsheet is true in life, too—everything matters, every decision, every choice. Often we won't know until much later why or how, but the things we do and say today shape our tomorrows.

Take my life. If I hadn't worked hard in elementary school, from when I was very young, I would never have been selected for the advanced program in middle school. If I hadn't succeeded there, I would not have been leapfrogged a year ahead at Jamaica High. If had I not chosen band as my music class elective, I would not have ended up sitting next to Brenda Moore.

If we hadn't met, I might not have heard the extra encouragement I needed to pursue college. If I hadn't listened to my academic adviser at the University of Buffalo, I would not have applied for an interview with representatives of the Big Eight accounting firms and started a career with Arthur

Andersen. And so on, through to becoming financially secure and set for life. So many small links along the way fashioned the chain of events of my life.

In the same way, what appeared to be just a small thing opened up a door to the new life God had for us after my strokes. Having appreciated so much the care I received while in the hospital and then going through rehabilitation at the Bridge, I wrote a brief letter to Barbara Doyle, the CEO of the hospital, telling her how highly I thought of her staff and how appreciative I was for their part in my recovery.

That led to an invitation to speak to a stroke support group about my experiences, about eighteen months after leaving the hospital. I was a little nervous, because I had never been one to draw attention to myself. I was confident about speaking in public, having done so often during the IPO "road shows," but that had been to talk about business, not me. Mom's admonition not to brag still rang in my ears. Yet I thought that I might be able to give others a shot in the arm through telling my story, and I knew how important it had been for me to hear encouraging words when I was in recovery.

I'd even tried to boost others' spirits when I was still in rehab, though with mixed results. Sometimes people thanked me. Then there was the man who came to the program when I was already about halfway through. He was a little older than me, probably in his early sixties, and struggling with the physical limitations incurred because of his stroke.

We were in the gym, a group of us balanced on large bouncy balls like we were in a kids' playground. It probably looked a bit comical to see all those adults sitting there like that, bouncing around the room, but the exercise was useful in helping us regain our equilibrium. The newcomer was having none of it, however, grumbling about how dumb the whole thing was.

"Hey, I know how you feel, believe me," I told him. "It seemed silly to me, too, when they first asked me to do it, but I've found that it is really helpful, you know. We've just got to do it."

My words seemed to fall on deaf ears, so I just let it go. I remembered days when I had been down in the dumps as well. I just hoped that he might remember what I said on another day, when he was feeling a bit brighter.

When someone contacted me on behalf of Barbara Doyle to thank me for my letter and ask me to speak to a group of recoverees and their loved ones, I didn't think twice. I went along and told them about what had happened to me, about the migraines and then ending up in the hospital, and my time in an induced coma. I told them about the great help I had received and how I'd been discouraged sometimes by what seemed to be a lack of progress in my recovery.

Tears filled my eyes as I recalled my encounter with God that night alone in my hospital room, when I surrendered and told Him that whatever He had for me was okay with me. The reality of that moment washed over me afresh as I spoke. I told them that even though I knew God was with me, I had still been scared about all the what-if questions. What if I didn't recover well? What if I never learned to walk without a cane?

Brenda, who had been with me at the meeting, turned to me on the drive home. "You never told me you were afraid, Tony."

I explained that I hadn't wanted to say so because to speak the words out loud somehow seemed like I was giving them room in my life to grow, like a weed. That conviction had been confirmed one Sunday morning not long after I came home from the hospital. I wasn't feeling up to going out to church yet, so I'd tuned in to a church service on the television. I found myself watching the service from Lakewood Church in Houston, Texas. Pastor Joel Osteen was preaching about dealing with doubts and worries. It was important not to say everything you thought, he had said, because that can make problems seem more real and therefore more difficult to overcome.

I recalled for Brenda how this message had sealed my silence about my fears. "I'd told God that I was going to trust Him come what may, so I was trying to do that by not asking questions," I said. "When I'd find my mind wandering off and asking what-ifs, I'd try to stop it. It was about giving up control.

"If you are going to trust, then you have to trust; it's as simple as that."

"You know," she told me, "you've really changed, Tony." She smiled. "In a good way."

It was good to hear she had noticed a difference. "I used to have to control everything," I admitted, "but I realized I can't, really."

Being less intently focused on what I had in mind, what I determined needed to be done, made me more aware of opportunities to do things for others. I began to get other invitations to speak to stroke groups about my experience, and I enjoyed being able to offer some encouragement and hope.

Sometimes, if I wasn't introduced as having suffered a stroke myself, I wouldn't let on right away. I'd offer some advice on recovery and prevention, and only at the conclusion of my remarks would I mention that, by the way, I'd suffered a stroke, just like them, and had been in their place, sitting in a wheelchair or having to use a walker. It was fun to see people shake their heads in disbelief and then draw some inspiration for their situation. After all, if I had been able to bounce back, why not them?

As part of my presentation, I'd pass on John Wooden's advice: remember the three Fs of faith, family, and friends. This gave me the opportunity to speak about how God had touched and transformed my life. I wouldn't ram my beliefs down anyone's throat, but to have left out the spiritual component that had been such an important part of my recovery would not have been really honest.

I knew how important it was to hear positive stories from people who were further down the recovery road. When I was going through rehabilitation, in addition to being diligent in doing my exercises, I read as much as I could about strokes and recovery. Lee and Bob Woodruff's book, *In an Instant: A Family's Journey of Love and Healing*, had been particularly inspiring. In it they told of the challenges they'd had to overcome after Bob was injured in Iraq in 2006, when an improvised explosive device, or IED, went off near the tank he was riding in while embedded with troops as co-anchor of ABC's *World News Tonight*.

Suffering a traumatic brain injury, Bob was kept in a medically induced coma for more than a month. His recovery had been more demanding than mine, including having to learn to walk and speak again. The way the couple had faced his health crisis together had been deeply touching, and Lee's devotion to her husband reminded me of how Brenda had supported me.

What a delight it was, then, to get to meet Lee in person when she came to share their recovery story with a support group at Fairfax Hospital.

As well as telling my personal story, I was also asked to take part in some medical symposiums. Doctors and other medical professionals would talk about stroke research and developments in care, and I would speak about my experiences as a patient. I'd talk about all the good things, the professionalism and personable nature of the staff, but also point out areas where I felt there was some room for improvement. For example, I didn't think the lead therapist had handled things well when she had tried to dissuade me from going back to work on finishing my time at the Bridge.

Invitations to be part of these kinds of events continue to this day. I've been asked to speak to many groups on behalf of the American Stroke Association and the American Heart Association, for whom I have been appointed a regional ambassador. I typically visit groups once or twice a month, recalling in my talks how in the early days after my strokes I couldn't walk or remember seven key words for ten or so minutes, how I had trouble balancing in the shower; and yet a few months later I was back at work and a year later I had completed a 5k.

It is so encouraging to me to be able to be an encouragement to others. I remember the days in my recovery when getting well seemed hard going or out of reach, and I needed someone to give me a boost. I love being able to cheer others on, to remind them that they can recover from a stroke and enjoy not just a full life, but even a better life because of what they can learn—about themselves, others, and God—if they are willing. If I can give someone else the inspiration they need to press on by sharing my story—some of which I have pieced together from what others have told me, as there's a chunk of time I simply do not remember—I count it a privilege.

Though I spend most of my time on the positives, I don't

ignore the downsides. After detailing my recovery and talking about all the things I have gained, I'll acknowledge what's been lost as well. While to all intents and purposes I'm one hundred percent better, that's not entirely true. My vision is impaired, and my left arm shakes a little at times, though most people would not notice.

Embracing and accommodating these kinds of changes are crucial parts of what I call "accepting the new normal." But I consider them to be just minor inconveniences, given the ways things could have turned out.

Having said that, coming to this place is essential. The therapists at the Bridge emphasized that only when we could come to acceptance of what had happened would we then begin to find the hope needed for recovery. Without resolving that, we'd never have the determination to look ahead, they said; we'd always be hankering for what was.

I recognized the truth of what they were saying, but for me it goes further; rather than acceptance and hope, I prefer to speak about surrender and faith—the added dimension that is opened up when we allow God into the situation. I didn't just accept what had happened to me; I surrendered to God's plans and purposes. I didn't just have hope that things might work out in the future; I had and continue to have faith that with God's help, they would.

When I speak, I also pass along what I hope is some helpful advice. I talk about working hard at recovery, but at the same time recognizing where you need to adapt to the new situation, as I did. For instance, I learned to "scan" to compensate for my peripheral vision, and I'm more careful about filling a glass of water or a cup of coffee that I am going to carry in my weaker left hand, knowing it is more prone to being spilled.

I remind them that they need other people on their team in their recovery, because they will not always be aware of the ways they have been affected, or of the progress they are making, because they are too close to it. You truly don't know what you don't know, and you need others to point it out to you.

"You have to get naked," I say, explaining that accepting your vulnerability is essential. I recall how I agreed to have Brenda sit in on all my therapy sessions, seeing me at my weakest and most vulnerable. Part of being naked is also facing, owning, and talking about the different emotions you experience, getting it all out in the open so everyone knows where you are in your journey. Recovery is not a straightforward rising line; it dips and goes back up again as we have bad days and good, setbacks and successes.

It's vital to acknowledge how one day we may feel confident and grateful, and the next discouraged and fearful. There may be anger about what has happened, sadness about what has been lost, frustration at seemingly slow progress in recovery, anxiety about the future. Identifying and acknowledging feelings takes some of the power away from them.

I got through my anger pretty quickly, thankfully, that first night I was left alone in the hospital after coming out of my induced coma. By God's grace, I was able to let that go and move forward.

But having gotten over the self-important idea that I didn't deserve what had happened to me, I then struggled for a while with the idea that maybe I *did* deserve it. Looking back on my life, I had to admit to myself that there were things that I regretted, times when I had not lived up to what I really believed deep down.

Regret and guilt are dangerous places to get stuck, because

believing that you somehow deserve to be in the situation in which you find yourself will limit your ability to hope that things can change and will weaken your determination to work hard so they do.

Thankfully, I was lifted out of my doubts by something I read on social media. Someone observed how flawed some of the great characters of the Bible had been: Noah got drunk, Jacob was a cheat, Moses got angry, Rahab was a prostitute, and David was an adulterer who plotted a murder. Yet each was used mightily by God.

It was encouraging for me to be reminded of this, a lesson that was hammered home soon afterward in a Sunday sermon at Antioch Baptist Church. The senior pastor there, Rev. Dr. Marshal L. Ausberry, told everyone, "You can't out-sin God's grace."

Though faith has seen me through all the storms, I don't want to pretend that it's all been clear sailing. I'd be lying if I told you that there have not been times when I have doubted God or questioned His goodness. But thankfully these have been brief troughs, and something I have read, something someone has said, a song I have heard, or something Dr. Ausberry has preached has revived my belief and trust and hope.

Another important feeling you might need to recognize is shame, the sense that having a stroke is something to be embarrassed about for some reason. Indeed, for the first year or so after my brush with death, I'd refer to what happened to me as "a blood clot." Only after my DVT scare did I begin to talk openly about strokes: I decided that I had no reason to hide what had happened to me, and if by telling others I could prevent similar occurrences, it was worth being open.

"Don't accept that there's a stigma attached to having suffered a stroke," I now tell people. "It's nothing to be embarrassed about or ashamed of. It happens to around eight hundred thousand people every year! You are not alone."

Sometimes Brenda comes with me to these support group meetings and will share her perspective as a caregiver. Having cared for others in difficult times as a nurse, Brenda found herself on the receiving end as I lay in a coma. People often say how difficult the strokes must have been for me, but she had it much tougher: I was unaware of everything for a long time!

From her experience, Brenda emphasizes the importance of caregivers having family and friends to lean on. They can be not only a source of strength and help to the caregiver, but also a valuable presence for the patient when the caregiver needs a break.

"It's so important for someone to *be there* with the patient as much as possible," she says. "Even if they may not seem to be aware of you, I believe it does count for something on a subconscious level. It says that you are there and that you care, that you haven't given up on them."

In that regard, Brenda was also especially appreciative of the many hospital staff who made a point of addressing me when they were checking on me or tending me in some way, speaking to me by name as if I could hear. And she appreciated being given explanations of the different procedures that were being performed, communicating that I wasn't just a patient, a task, but that I was still a person, an individual.

On the road to recovery, Brenda speaks about the importance of being the quiet, dependable support. She recalls how she did not have the same kind of lows I experienced on occasion because she could more clearly see the progress I was making, while sometimes I was so focused on the tree I was trying to climb that I could not stand back and see the forest.

Together we tell couples how important it is that they

become a team. That doesn't mean you always have to agree on everything, but you do need to work hard to make sure you understand each other. And you need to be careful not to unwittingly keep each other in the dark: by way of illustration, we tell how when I was in my coma, Brenda had been unable to access our bank account online because I'd handled that responsibility and was the only one who knew the pass code.

While I speak about how important the act of surrendering was in my recovery, I also emphasize something that seems to be paradoxical: the vital part our own effort plays. But these two things are not contradictory. Rather, they are like the long pole high-wire walkers carry; when the pole is held properly, the opposite ends provide the right balance that keeps you from falling. Once you have trusted everything to God, your part is then just to do everything asked of you and leave the results to Him.

As I recall how I threw myself wholeheartedly into my recovery program, I admit to a secret vow I had made to myself while I was working on my motor skills: that I would not fall over. Perhaps it was a bit of the old pride still inside me, but I just didn't want to end up flat on my face or my back. I was determined to stay upright come what may, and this inner determination helped to keep me motivated. Though I had a few serious wobbles, I never did completely fall during my recovery.

On one speaking engagement, when I mentioned this, a hand went up in the group.

"But what about that time in the hospital with your friend Mike, on Father's Day?" the person said. "Didn't you fall on your face on the bed then?"

I had to laugh; he had me there. "Technically, I guess you could say that that was a fall," I replied with a smile. "But I like to think of it more as a consequence of not following the right procedure. When I was doing things the way I had been told, from walking to running to going up and down stairs, I never fell once."

My speaking appearances include practical advice. For example, I caution people against thinking about driving again too soon. I know it's an important measure of independence, but I warn them not to rush into it. I didn't start driving again for a year after my strokes, and to this day I have careful boundaries in place. I won't drive in bad weather at night, because my vision is slightly impaired in those conditions. I also try to make sure not to spend more than two hours behind the wheel at a time, because scanning to compensate for my lost vision is tiring. If I don't think I should drive, I'll ask Brenda to or get a car service: it's not worth endangering yourself and others just to feel more independent.

When I do drive, I try to make sure I am in the left-hand lane, as much as possible, because this reduces the need for me to rely on scanning to compensate for the lost peripheral vision on that side. And I avoid highways as much as I can; no need to put myself in the midst of fast-moving traffic that's often switching lanes without warning. With GPS readily available on our smart phones, taking secondary routes is easy; it just means allowing a little extra travel time.

Actually, this is a lesson that can be applied to all areas of life: add some margin. Do whatever you can to reduce the stress. It may mean getting somewhere more slowly or taking longer to complete a task, but so be it. At the end of the day, is it worth getting worked up about a few lost minutes? In the light of all that you could have lost because of a stroke, these kind of adjustments are pretty inconsequential.

By telling my story, I also hope to play a small part in raising awareness about the important issue of strokes. They are a major health challenge in the United States, killing around 130,000 people every year—that's one person every four minutes or so. Strokes account for one in twenty deaths and leave many others seriously incapacitated for the rest of their lives, which in turn brings financial and emotional burdens. Strokes are estimated to cost America around thirty-four billion dollars annually, including healthcare, medication, and missed work.

With all that in mind, I emphasize two things in my presentations: prevention and reaction. Some strokes, like mine, come without warning, but there are things we can do to minimize the likelihood of having one, primarily by taking better care of ourselves. High blood pressure, high cholesterol, diabetes, obesity, smoking, and drinking too much all heighten your risk of stroke.

When someone does have a stroke, I remind people, a FAST response is essential in minimizing the damage, especially if they have already had one stroke, which puts them at higher risk of another. The acronym spells out the warning signs to look for:

F is for *face*: is it droopy at all? Can you smile? A is for *arms*: are they tingly or feeling heavy? Can you raise them both above your head? S is for *speech*: do you sound slurry, or is it difficult to find the right words? T is for *time*: none to lose, and time to call 911! The faster a stroke can be identified and treated, the greater the possibility of reducing its impact. Get to the hospital right away.

And finally, before inviting questions, I encourage people to do all they can to reduce their risk by eating healthy and exercising. The sobering fact is that doctors estimate that around eighty percent of all strokes can be avoided by people taking better care of their health.

Many times in Q and A sessions I am asked whether it's helpful for people to visit someone who has had a stroke and might be asleep or otherwise unaware that a visitor is with them. I always encourage them to go, for two reasons.

First, you never know what patients are aware of in their environment, even though they seem to be out of it. After my stay in the hospital, more and more memories of people visiting and speaking with me came back. I believe their presence was an encouragement to me, even if I could not register it then and there. And if a patient does sense your presence in any way, it's sure to be an encouragement. I know that having so many people come by to wish me well and tell me they were rooting for me really spurred me even further in my efforts to recover. Not only did I want to do everything I could for my own sake; I also didn't want to feel like I was letting them down.

Second, it is definitely a boost to a patient's family and loved ones to know that they have not been forgotten, either. Visits to us in Reston Hospital were a great encouragement to Brenda on the long days I was out of it.

While I hope people are encouraged by hearing my counsel and my story, at the same time I warn them to be careful about comparing themselves to me, or their situation to that of anyone else. That can easily lead to discouragement and disappointment.

One time a couple of years or so after my strokes, I went to speak to a group at John Hopkins Hospital in Baltimore, Maryland. Among the attendees was a woman just a little younger than me who had suffered a stroke around the same time I did.

But she had not recovered nearly as well and was still dealing with speech, memory, and mobility issues.

"Look at me compared to you," she said afterward. "I'm doing horribly."

I felt for her in her disappointment and frustration. "We just have to trust God," I told her sympathetically. "We don't know what His plan is in all of this, for you or for me. We don't know what He wants to use you for. Maybe He has something different for you. That doesn't make it better or worse; it's just different." I told her how I'd had to surrender control to God, telling Him that I was fine with whatever He had in store for me. And I encouraged her to try to do the same.

More recently I was speaking to another stroke support group when a lady there simply couldn't believe that I had been in such poor condition, because I had recovered so fully. "That's just not possible," she declared, after I described the severity of my strokes, and my recovery.

"You're right," I agreed. "Humanly, it's not possible. But the Bible says that with God, all things are possible. He made it happen."

CHAPTER 11

"I JUST WASN'T LISTENING"

For some people to be able to bounce back so well, like me, and for others to have long-term struggles with the aftermath of a stroke can seem unfair, I know. Some people ask me whether I'd be as positive as I am had I not made such a nearly full recovery. It's a fair question.

I believe, in all honesty, that the answer is yes, I would. That night when I told God I would accept whatever He brought my way, I meant it with all of my heart. Yes, I got frustrated and discouraged at times along the way after that, but deep down I knew that He was ultimately in control and I needed to embrace that.

While some people experience a personality change after they suffer a stroke, it was not so much the case with me. I still believe in being on time for everything—in fact, at least fifteen minutes early, if possible—and most days you will still find me in a suit and tie, even though I no longer go to my own office. For me, the change has been in my identity. No longer am I defined by what *I do*; now I am defined by what *God has done for me*.

It's all about perspective. Dr. Ausberry helped sum it up for me in one of his sermons, after my recovery. He talked about how we don't like to deal with storms in life but how sometimes they aren't a bad thing. In fact, God sometimes uses them to take us somewhere we might not otherwise have gone, like Jonah in the Bible.

When God told Jonah to go and preach to the people of Nineveh, he so disliked the idea that he ran away, jumping a ship bound for Tarshish. When a big storm came up, the crew pitched Jonah into the sea, where he was swallowed by a big fish. Subsequently spat up onto the beach, a chastened Jonah finally took God's message of love to the people of Nineveh.

I'm not saying that storms are always the result of our dis-obedience, but when bad things happen, the question really isn't, *Why me?* It's, *Why not me?* And then, *What do you want me to do with this, God?*

That's certainly been true for me, and I would not swap the life I have now, knowing God as I do, for anything that came before. Indeed, a friend has joked that I should refer to my life prior to May 12, 2007, as BS: Before Surrender! What at first seemed to be the worst day in my life I now look back on as the best, as it gave me a fresh start.

Actually, often when I talk about what happened, I don't even refer to it as "my strokes" anymore. Instead, I speak of "my experience with God." My life was changed not by a stroke of fate, as some would have it, but by what I call a stroke of faith. That's the defining point for me.

There have been places along the way in my recovery that stood out as mile markers, moments when I really knew that I was making progress. One was getting back to my desk at Sego-via; picking up on some of my old responsibilities made my recovery seem more real, in some ways: it was clear evidence that I still had what it takes. And yet, returning to work also took it out of me.

Heeding my therapists' advice, I started with three-hour days, going in at about nine a.m. and working until noon. Any doubts I may have had about being too cautious were soon dispelled—I was exhausted by the time I was ready to go home. Though I could do all that I had previously, the various activities took much more concentration as my brain continued to heal.

Brenda drove me to and from the office. I'd been warned while still in rehab not to consider taking the wheel right away, and I followed that advice. Having lost most of the peripheral vision on my left side, I was still learning how to compensate for that by "scanning," actively turning my head a lot to take in the view. It was only a small movement, but repeated so consistently it did get tiring.

Much as I knew letting Brenda drive me everywhere was wise, it took some getting used to. Maybe it's just a guy thing, but I'd always been behind the wheel: I liked being in the driver's seat. Switching places in the car with Brenda became something of a metaphor for other changes in our relationship after my strokes.

Though we had started out with equal commitment to our work and careers when we got married, through the years we had defaulted to a more traditional arrangement. It just seemed to make sense, what with pregnancy and childbirth, plus the financial rewards I was reaping. So over time I became the breadwinner and Brenda was the stay-at-home mom.

We accepted our situation happily and were content in our marriage, but we were not aware of how in assuming those roles, we also fell into a way of doing life that was not as rich as it might be, for us and our family. My long hours meant that I missed a lot of small but significant moments in our children's lives—something that I had begun to try to correct in the couple of years or so before my strokes, though there was still room for improvement.

Though work was often on my mind when I was at home, meaning sometimes I could be there in body but not in spirit, I tended not to talk to Brenda about the opportunities and challenges we were facing at the office. I'd tell her when a big decision was made but usually would not involve her in the process as I figured things out.

That approach had led to one amusing incident during my recovery in the hospital. In the early days after I came around after my lost month, Brenda had been encouraged to gently engage me in conversation, asking lots of questions to help gauge how much my memory had been affected.

Having asked me the names of loved ones, and details about where we lived and where I worked, she added, "So, do you remember buying a private plane?"

"Yeah," I told her. "I remember that. Why?"

"Well, you never told me about any plane," she responded emphatically. "I didn't know you had a plane!"

It wasn't that I had been hiding it from her; I just hadn't thought to bother her with what seemed like mere office details. As Segovia continued to take off, Mike and I had found ourselves having to travel to some out-of-the-way places to meet with prospective and new Department of Defense clients. Getting there and back in a day on commercial airlines was proving impossible, and we were losing too many hours traveling when our time was at a premium. We decided that buying fractional ownership in a plane, pilot and all, made the best business sense. We ended up with about one-sixteenth of a private jet—though, of course, we were glad to have all of it for the time we were using it!

Brenda became aware of all this only while I was still in a coma. When Mike visited the hospital one day as Brenda waited at my bedside, she mentioned to him how some of my family in New York wanted to visit but were having trouble with the long drive.

"No problem," Mike said, to her surprise. "Mark and I have this private plane. I'll send it up to New York to get them and fly them back here."

Mike had also come to the rescue with another situation that arose during the long days I was unconscious, which also revealed how Brenda and I were leading fairly parallel lives.

In keeping with the way we carried our different responsibilities, I handled all the domestic finances. You might argue that as a household responsibility it should have fallen under Brenda's watch, but I was the accountant, after all, so it was easier and quicker for me to do it. I had everything well organized, as you might expect, with electronic deposits and payments set up.

The only trouble was, with me incapacitated and the only one who knew our online pass codes, Brenda could not get into our account to authorize debits. She could see that money was going into our account, but she could not access it. In the end, she explained the problem to Mike and he canceled my direct-debit payment and cut her a physical check so she could pay it into another account we had and use that one to pay all the bills that were coming in.

My strokes upset our domestic arrangement, and in a good way. I found myself having to rely on Brenda more for all sorts of things, while she felt more freedom to speak up and offer her perspective and opinion. We both found we were enjoying the way that our relationship was growing and changing as a result of the challenges we faced—the situation drew us together in our shared need, first, and then forced us to reallocate our responsibilities and involvement in coming up with the solutions. I discovered that I liked talking things through with her in a way that we hadn't always done before.

Not that renegotiating the balance of our relationship was always easy. Overwhelmingly, I was grateful beyond words to Brenda for her devotion and support. She was always there for me, putting her wishes and other commitments to one side to give herself totally to my recovery. But there were a few times when her concern bugged me a bit.

One such area surrounded my preparation for the 5k. I did a lot of training on the treadmill in our basement, and my running style, especially in the early days, certainly looked a bit inelegant to an observer. In fact, my gait was so awkward that we actually had to trade out the treadmill we had before my strokes for one with a wider track, to accommodate my foot placement. My step was so wide that I kept partially hitting the side of the treadmill by the moving track, risking a stumble.

With the new machine in place, I'd step up onto the treadmill, fire up my gospel playlist, and get started. Then I'd feel something behind me. Brenda would come by and put her hand in the waist of my pants to hold me steady, because she feared I would fall. This really irritated me, making me feel like I was a little boy who needed his hand held. It took several conversations for us to be able to work it through.

"Please, Bren, let go," I'd tell her. "I'm okay. Just let me get my balance and run on my own here."

"But you look like you are going to fall at any moment."

"I get it, honey," I'd say. "I look a bit wobbly, I know. But this is part of the process. And I'm just not gonna get there if you keep holding on to my pants like that."

"I was just trying to help," she would say, hurt.

"I know, Bren, I know. But you need to let go, okay? I know anything can happen, but I promise you I am not going to fall."

Of course, this give-and-take, learning to listen to each other, went both ways. As time went by and I stretched the hours I worked at Segovia to a longer day—I was full-time again within a month of returning—I began to hanker for the sense of independence that being able to drive myself about would bring. I told Brenda one day that I thought I was ready to start driving again.

"Oh no, you are not," she said definitely. "You're not ready for that yet, Tony, trust me. If you make a mistake out there you could kill yourself or you could kill someone else. It's just not worth the risk of rushing things."

Deep down, though I was disappointed to hear it, I knew that she was right. I repeated the Serenity Prayer, asking God for the wisdom to know what to accept and let go of. I stopped asking Brenda about driving again and decided to concentrate on appreciating her help more. And when the time did finally come when I got behind the wheel again, about a year and a half after I got out of hospital, I realized just how correct Brenda had been in her assessment.

In the months leading up to the first anniversary of my strokes, I practiced scanning, looking around constantly to compensate for my lost peripheral vision. Then, when Brenda agreed I was probably ready to start driving again, we'd go out to the nearest shopping mall, before the stores opened on Sunday morning, and I would practice maneuvers in the empty parking lot. It was tiring, taking every ounce of my greater concentration and improved energy, both of which would have been markedly less a few months earlier.

One of the richest ways in which our new life together began to change was through our shared experiences at church. The foundation of church as an important dimension of life had been laid early in both our childhoods and remained solid, but it was never much more than that. We had attended church fairly faithfully all through the years but had not really done much to build on the first building block of Sunday service.

We had settled at Antioch Baptist Church in Fairfax Station soon after making a home in Virginia. The people there were very welcoming and the messages and music were positive, reminding me of Cornerstone back in Brooklyn. But we had never really tried to get involved beyond Sunday morning—if I even attended then, rather than deal with a pressing business concern. Indeed, we had been so anonymous in our attendance that no one from the church ever made contact with Brenda or visited me in the hospital after my strokes—not because they didn't care, but because we hadn't made ourselves known to them.

That new, deeper awareness of God's reality and everyday presence in my life had remained with me ever since my encounter with Him in the hospital, soon after coming out of my induced coma. Its intensity had wavered at times when recovery seemed slow in coming, but I had never doubted the reality of what I had experienced. And, knowing more clearly and surely that God was there, I wanted to know about Him more clearly and surely.

We started by attending Wednesday night Bible study on a regular basis. On returning to Segovia I had adjusted my work schedule even after my energy levels were restored. Cutting back on my hours to a more manageable regular workday was not just about my health, but also about my other priorities. In the past, I'd dismissed the idea of getting to midweek Bible study because, as I saw it, I had more important things to do. Now it was simply the most important item on my agenda.

I loved discovering just how relevant the Bible was to everyday life. Truths like *God only gives you what He knows you can handle*, which I had found in 1 Corinthians, weren't rare flashes of wisdom, I realized. The Bible was full of direction, instruction, correction, and encouragement, if only I would give time to searching it out.

Maybe I was concentrating more on what was being said, but the Sunday sermons seemed to be more meaningful, too. I had always appreciated the way Dr. Ausberry preached. But now it was as though some of his messages were directed at me personally.

One Sunday early in my recovery we were at Antioch when I was having a bit of a hard time dealing with all that still lay ahead of me. I was questioning why things had happened the way they did, why as a healthy, middle-aged man, I'd been reduced to relearning things like how to tie my shoelaces and how to write a check.

That morning Dr. Ausberry spoke about the different ways God works and moves to get our attention. He said that people often asked him why God didn't speak to them in the way some others claimed He did. Well, God did speak to people, Dr. Ausberry went on—all the time—but sometimes it was in a whisper and they were not listening. So then sometimes God had to shout to get their attention.

As Brenda drove us home afterward, I said to her, "Well, if what Pastor Ausberry said this morning doesn't explain 2007, I don't know what else does."

Brenda looked over at me, waiting for me to go on. "I mean, I think God's been talking to me for years," I said. "I just wasn't listening. I was too busy running my own life."

It came down to this, I realized, as I thought about it some more: I had been too busy living in the *world*, when I should have been living more in the *Word*—the Bible and all God had to speak to me about through it. There is only a small difference between the two words, but at the same time the gap between the two, the shift in focus, is immense. My life was similar, I reflected.

Outwardly, I had probably seemed like a nice guy to most people, before the stroke. I didn't cheat on my taxes. I was committed to my family and conscientious in my work. I demanded the best of people, but I didn't expect things they were incapable of. I treated everyone with respect, whatever their position. I tried to be generous, often helping out family and friends who were in need, without expecting anything in return.

Much of that came from the strong internal compass that had been embedded in me from my childhood. The thing with a compass bearing, however, is that when you first set out, being off by a fraction of a degree doesn't really matter. The farther you go, though, the more widely you veer off course, bit by bit. After half a century of doing things my way, I was not where I should be, I realized.

It wasn't that I was a really bad person—I just wasn't good enough. Yes, I'd been able to achieve a lot in part because of my own drive and determination, but that only allowed me to make the most of the gifts and abilities God has given me in the first place. And I hadn't stopped to consider how He might want me to apply them.

My strokes had brought me to an abrupt halt, interrupting my foot-on-the-pedal approach to life. Then the process of recovery had forced me to be slower about everything, allowing more time for reflection, thought, and prayer.

I was grateful for having been forced to slow down in this way: recognizing now how God had been trying to get my attention, I was determined not to miss His direction anymore. I felt like I was embarking on a new journey, one that I was strangely content not to be in control of.

Ironically, letting go of things only seemed to increase the success I enjoyed in business. Going back to Segovia, I knew that I wanted to reduce the amount of time I gave to work, but not the effort I put in while I was there. Mike had carried a double load while I was out of commission, and I did not expect him to continue to cover for me.

But I did begin to let go of some things and start to delegate. In fact, this became another growth area for me, learning how good leadership involves finding the right people and then giving them the room and the tools to grow. That meant not being a micromanager, which had been a bit of a tendency of mine previously.

Mike and I took time to assess where things were with Segovia. We'd flown under the radar to begin with, picking up small contracts here and there that were not of interest to larger businesses. Over time, as these contracts were renewed and expanded and others were added, we had built an operation that secured us each a seven-figure salary and a rising profile in the developing new communications world.

In late 2009 we hired a group to explore a sale of Segovia. They found potential buyers who required a close look at our books, doubtless hoping to find something of concern they might use as leverage to drive down our asking price. I was familiar with this from my days back at Arthur Andersen and had no worries that they would succeed. Our bookkeeping was solid.

Despite this, they did come back and make a reduced offer, on the basis that because many of our government contracts were financed from supplemental agencies, continued funding was uncertain. It was a clever argument, but one we refuted: everyone knew that was how the military world operated. We knew we had good cash flow and strong prospects, so we politely declined their offer, much to the surprise of our broker.

The following day I got a call from an old friend, Brad Busse, whom I knew from my days back with USA Mobile. He had been involved with our IPO, and we kept in touch from time to time.

"Did you sell your company yet?"

I told him no and explained that we had actually turned down an offer just twenty-four hours previously.

"Well, that's interesting," he said. "I think I may have someone who might be interested in your company."

When we met with the owners of this new prospect, they asked what we wanted for Segovia. They countered with an offer that was lower than the original price from the group that had previously been interested. We declined again, and both sides agreed to sit on it and think about things. Mike and I were still in no hurry.

About a month later, the CEO called again.

"We've thought about it, and how about we do this," he said in a conference call with Mike and me, recalling our asking price and their offer. "What do you say we meet in the middle?" This was more than we'd been offered to date.

We told him we needed to think about it and would get back to him. After hanging up, I looked at Mike and smiled. "Now, just to be clear," I said, knowing we had played hardball before, "we are going to take this deal, right?"

He nodded. "Oh yes, we are," he told me. "But not right away. We don't want to look like we are desperate. We'll call back tomorrow."

And so Segovia was acquired by Inmarsat, a mobile satellite operator based in London, England. I took a deep breath the day our bank called and told me that the big wire transfer had just hit our account. I had dealt with large sums of money before, but not ones with such a personal impact. The sale had made me wealthier than I had ever imagined—but not without some conditions. The acquisition comprised a large cash payment up front, with almost half as much again on meeting some agreed growth goals. Both Mike and I would be staying on with the company for the time being, but as employees rather than owners.

With the incentive of money still on the table, there was no time for slacking off. I threw myself into the new configuration with my usual commitment, but at the same time with the understanding that my twelve-hour days and always-available style were over.

Even with a reduced work focus, business continued to expand. Our additional payment was dependent on growth targets that were to be met within three years, but we achieved them within two. Mike and I received the extra money a year ahead of schedule. Because we'd overachieved, Inmarsat invited Mike and me to take the lead in some further acquisitions. But

I wasn't sure that I had it in me to re-up for the sort of time needed to see a new project through.

"To be honest, I don't know that I want to do this for another five years," I told Mike.

"If you're not doing it, then neither am I," he said.

I felt bad; we had been through a lot together, becoming like business battle buddies. He'd had my back through some hard times, and I didn't want him to miss out on opportunities for more success because of me.

"You don't need to do that," I said. "I just want to be fair to them, and I don't think it's right to say yes to something when I am not sure I am going to be able to see it through."

"No, Mark," Mike said. "If you're not doing it, I'm not. We started this thing together; we'll finish it together."

Though I increasingly sensed that my future lay elsewhere, for the first time I wasn't going to make a big business decision and then report back to Brenda. I wanted her help in reaching a conclusion—a further sign of the way we were weaving our lives together in a new way.

At home we talked about the money we had made and the new money that was being offered.

"That's a lot of money, Bren," I said. "But how much does someone really need? I think enough's enough, don't you?" She agreed.

The idea of retiring at the age of little more than fifty seemed strange at first. I knew, though, that it wasn't going to mean playing golf every day or just sitting around checking on my investments. God had been changing me, bit by bit, but He was working with the raw materials of the life I gave Him, rather than sweeping them away and replacing them with new parts.

I was still a type A kind of person, though hopefully tempered more and more by God's Spirit. I still wanted to achieve things, but now for Him, rather than me. I wanted other people to come to experience more of His presence and peace, just as I had—and hopefully without having to go through what I did to get there.

Looking back, I realized that, prior to my strokes, I would probably have defined myself, gratefully, as a wealthy man, in part because of what I had been prepared to do. But since my time in the hospital, I had come to realize that, in a way much more important than simple wealth, I was a rich man—not in a financial sense, and not because of anything I had ever done.

I wanted to spend the rest of my life helping others make the same discovery.

CHAPTER 12

"WE NEVER FORGOT"

Whenever I get to tell my story, I make a point of noting that, actually, it isn't just mine. Any major life event, be it wonderful or tragic, affects not only the individual concerned, but also all those around him, loved ones and friends. It's like when you throw a stone into a pond—the ripples spread outward.

In the same way, my strokes impacted not only my life, but the lives of others as well. They changed us as a couple and as a family. Brenda and I are closer than ever. This is a real gift, because many couples who have to deal with a major trauma are overwhelmed by the pressures and conflict that can result.

I had always assumed that a major crisis like a stroke would draw a couple together, uniting them in the storm, but as I learned at the Bridge, that is not always the case: the struggle often drives them apart. Divorce is not uncommon among couples who go through a major crisis like a significant stroke.

Having been together since we were childhood sweethearts, I thought Brenda and I knew each other just about as well as possible, but we have both discovered new things as a result of my being sick that have been a delight.

Brenda says there's a new softness about me. I'm still that type A guy who likes things to add up, but she has seen a willingness to let go of *always* needing to be in control. Looking back, I can see that there were times when I was pretty unyielding, but now I am able to say, "You know, you might be right."

What I used to see as Brenda just being too emotional, I now welcome as a gift. I'm learning not always to lead just with my head, but to give my heart room to speak as well. Looking back, I can see that while being firm and decisive at work may have been the best way, it isn't always best in other areas and other relationships. I am learning to be less quick to come to hard-and-fast judgments.

Being weak and in need was difficult for me at first. I felt exposed, not the in-charge guy Brenda had married, but I came to accept it. As a result, I saw strengths and abilities coming out in Brenda that previously she'd not exercised, in part because of the way we had settled into our roles and responsibilities. Her having to step into different areas showed us that she could do it, and I didn't always need to be the one to.

I put it this way: we were always headed in the same direction, but now it's in a different formation. Previously, we were on two separate bicycles, rolling along side by side, but in parallel. Together but separate in a way. Now we're on a tandem, pedaling together, and it's much more fun.

One of the most rewarding changes has been how we have grown closer spiritually. Like me, Brenda had always believed in God, but as my faith had been crowded out by work, hers had been second to caring for the family. Both rather private people by nature—remember, we'd first started to really share our feelings by writing each other notes in high school—we'd never really talked much with each other about our own relationship with God.

Sharing that aspect of our lives more has been so enriching. I was moved to hear how Brenda had felt God's comfort and closeness wrapped around her like a blanket during my time in an induced coma, days when she didn't know whether she would get her husband back. That experience continues to inspire her to want to know more about Him.

I was amazed to learn how God used her in a pivotal way in my recovery. After coming out of my lost month and seeing Brenda for the first time, I'd initially been disappointed and hurt when she left me alone in my hospital room so soon. But then, in the quiet, I'd had that encounter with God that was in many ways the start of my new life, of letting go. Only much later did Brenda tell me that she'd felt prompted to go home, that I needed some alone time with God. How right she proved to be!

She has her own stories of experiencing God's comfort and care during my days in the hospital. Though Mike and Teresa and others were a tremendous help, there were times when she had only God to lean on.

Brenda and I celebrated our growing closer spiritually in a special way in 2015, on a trip to the Holy Land with a group from our church. It was amazing to visit so many historic spots, to literally walk in the footsteps of our Savior, and have the Bible come to life before our eyes. Even more wonderful was to follow Him down into the river Jordan together and be baptized as a symbol of our new life, and to renew our wedding vows in a special ceremony at Jerusalem's Church of the Holy Sepulcher, built on the traditional site of Jesus's burial.

Disentangling more and more from work at Segovia and

then finally selling the business also allowed Brenda and me to get involved at Antioch. We started with the midweek Bible study, where I began to love digging deeper into the Scriptures. But we didn't want to simply receive more for ourselves without giving something away.

We began by getting involved with the youth ministry, knowing how important the right influences can be during the teenage and young adult years. Neither Brenda nor I see ourselves as qualified or equipped to lead the programs, but we can come alongside as a sort of surrogate mom and pop, being around at all the events to provide a watchful eye, offering a listening ear at times, and of course helping with the fuel that drives youth programs—providing the food and snacks. We enjoy getting to be a small part of what's going on in the young lives at Antioch.

We also signed up to be part of the team at the church's welcome center. Antioch's membership is around two thousand, so it's easy for newcomers to feel a bit overwhelmed by the size and scope of everything that goes on, and we want them to feel welcomed. First-timers are invited over to the welcome center following the service to find out more about Antioch. We introduce ourselves, offer them coffee and cookies, and tell them a little about all that the church is involved in.

Away from Antioch, Brenda and I appreciate getting to spend more time with each other. We even go and have pedicures together, because I know how much she enjoys them, though our philanthropic work doesn't leave a lot of time for sitting around. It's just good to know the other is close by at home, even if we are working on different things. Nearly losing my life made me so much more aware of the preciousness of time, and how things can change in an instant.

Brenda and I are thankful for all the time we get to spend with Jenée and Markus, who, though adults with their own lives, still seem to enjoy hanging with Mom and Dad. In some ways, it's making up a little for some of what we missed along the way. Family life has become so much more precious. Family was always important to me; I just got my priorities a bit mixed up for longer than I should have, confusing providing with being present. I'm grateful to have the opportunity to correct that now.

Part of that family joy comes from grandparenthood. Jenée married Gerald Padmore on August 3, 2013, and they gave us Julian on November 21, 2014. Thankfully, they live just twenty minutes away, so we get to see plenty of them. I love nothing more than sitting with Julian on my lap, watching Elmo on the television. At the time of this writing, Brenda and I are excitedly awaiting the arrival of grandchild number two.

As Jenée and Gerald pursue their own professional dreams as a young couple, I make a point of urging them not to get so focused on work that they lose sight of home. "Don't miss those special moments, like I did," I tell them. They are gracious enough to smile when I lecture like that.

My health crisis pushed Jenée into adulthood in some ways. She really grew up taking on responsibility for making sure life was as normal as possible at home for Markus, while Brenda was camped out at the hospital. Like her mom and me, she found God in a deeper way. Prayer became alive, too. "God is always listening," she says. "He's always there. He's the greatest therapist, the best counselor ever—and He's free, which is great!"

Though Jenée was a wonderful surrogate mom for Markus, he was hit hard by my strokes. Even though he towered over me as a teenager, he still looked up to me. Watching me collapse in public outside the Hallmark store had been shocking. Seeing me subsequently incapacitated, the man who had always known what to do and had an answer for everything, really shook him—so much that he rarely came to see me while I was in the hospital because it was too upsetting.

Brenda and I did our best to shelter him from it all, even when I got home from the hospital. But people don't communicate only through words—they say things with their bodies, even when their lips are closed.

He's actually now almost grateful for what happened. "Daddy," he tells me—the affectionate name he still uses, unashamedly—"the stroke was a terrible thing, but in a way it kind of brought us all closer together more than anything else could have. It's like, we're all in this together."

Markus and I are bonded not only through our longtime shared love of sports, but also through my entering more into his world. Markus is interested in politics and journalism, and I love to sit and discuss issues of the day with him. Initially a little surprised by my seemingly sudden interest in God and faith, over the years he has seen that it is a deep part of who I am now, not just a phase.

"I know that you worked hard in recovery, but in my mind, there's no way you could have done that without the Lord Himself being on your side," he says. "I really feel like you had God on your shoulder, helping you get through all this. And while I may not be the most spiritual person, I do realize that: there's no way that you could have done all this without God on your side."

There is lots of laughter in our home. Sometimes, when I

mix up my words or stumble over something, as anyone might do, not directly because of my strokes, I'll still play the ill-health card and joke, "Hey, give me a break, I have a traumatic brain injury, you know." Or Jenée or Markus might teasingly call me "Strokeman."

The ripples of change go beyond our immediate family. I continue to honor my parents' wishes and look out for my siblings. Like all families, we have our differences, our misunderstandings, and our little quirks, but in our own way, we try to be there for one another.

I was touched to learn how many people had dropped whatever they were doing to get to the hospital when I underwent surgery. And I have also never forgotten those envelopes that arrived sporadically when I was scraping by as a student at the University of Buffalo—my family digging deep into their pockets to help me realize an opportunity that was not theirs.

After selling Segovia in 2010, Brenda and I knew of a couple of things we wanted to do with some of all that money. First, we paid for almost a hundred family members to join us on a four-day cruise, to celebrate our good fortunate and thank them for their love and support through my recovery.

Then, at Thanksgiving that year, we gathered with all the close family for a brunch on a visit to New York City; we always try to be sure to get everyone together when we are back there, often sometime between Mother's Day and Father's Day, when as many of us as possible will go out to Calverton National Cemetery to visit our parents' graves and remember them.

During the Thanksgiving brunch, both Brenda and I got up and spoke to everyone. We explained how we had sold the business and done well. Then we passed out envelopes to everyone there: our siblings and their partners, nephews and nieces, god-children, and four longtime close friends. There were some wide eyes and surprised expressions when people pulled out the sizable checks that were inside. Why were we doing this? they asked.

"It's what Mom taught us to do, remember? It's who she wanted us to be," I explained. "And remember when I was in Buffalo after Mom had passed, and Dad couldn't afford to help me anymore because of all the bills? I never asked, but you sent those envelopes with cash in them.

"It was a long time ago, but Brenda and I never forgot. You helped us get where we are today, and we will always be grateful for that."

My physical recovery mirrored the way I grew into what I consider to be my second life. I took baby steps to start with, unsure on my feet, as I gained more strength and confidence. Similarly, my walk with God became steadier, and as it did so I got a clearer idea of what I should do with the years ahead.

As I have mentioned, Brenda and I had always tried to be generous, first to family and then to others we knew of who had needs, but our help was kind of random. Through our strokes experience, we learned about other opportunities to make a difference in people's lives. The first couple were with the Bridge. We had already been invited to share our story with recovery groups, and then the hospital administration came to us with a request. Would we fund the purchase of a couple of pieces of important equipment for the rehab program? They wanted to buy a driving simulator to replace the old, basic computer program they were using, and they wanted to purchase a swallow station, a machine that could identify how a stroke has affected a person's throat and his or her ability to drink and eat—a far more sophisticated technique than the eat-a-peanut-butter-cracker test used for me.

We were pleased to write checks for both of them. It was the biggest amount of money we had ever donated, but we were thrilled to do so, happy to be able to visualize just how both pieces of equipment would help people who were in the same circumstances we had been in.

Not long afterward, Brenda and I were invited to lunch by the president of the Inova Health Foundation, which includes Mount Vernon among its hospitals. Also there was Barbara Doyle, to whom I had written my letter of appreciation. I knew we were going to be asked to make a donation, and I had no problem with that. I nearly choked when I heard the amount, though.

Our host explained that the foundation wanted to build a new tower with private rooms at Mount Vernon. Right away I knew that was a good plan, remembering my time sharing a room with the patient who could not make it to the bathroom at night. Maintaining patients' privacy and dignity as much as possible is really important, especially when each is being intruded upon unavoidably in so many ways in their treatment.

Then our host asked whether we would consider donating an amount with a long row of zeroes in it—many times more than what we'd given to the Bridge. Though I was surprised, I was not offended—indeed, I kind of admired the man's straightforwardness and courage. I told him we would need to discuss the request.

It didn't take long. "Tell him we'll do it," Brenda said when we got to the car.

"Really?" I responded, defaulting to my accountant mode. "Just like that?"

"Yes," she said. "Look, Tony, you were a patient here yourself. The hospitals did a wonderful job for us. We know that. We can afford the amount. We need to do it."

We called that night and told him the check would be on its way. We also agreed to become the lead donors for the project, which in its own way was an even bigger stretch for us. Giving a big sum of money was one thing, but having our names out there in public was another. This was never the way I had operated, always preferring to be a behind-the-scenes kind of guy. But I understood that it was a good fund-raising strategy—putting a human face to a project makes it much more relatable, much more attractive to others to consider getting involved too.

While we didn't want or need any public credit for our part, if having our names out there helped generate more support, we were willing to do it. This was another way in which I felt God was stretching me out of my old comfort zone. We also sponsored two galas that doubled our sizable initial gift. In due course, Brenda and I would be among the special guests at the official dedication of the Mark and Brenda Moore Patient Tower, with its private rooms and state-of-the-art facilities.

The way we agreed to support the hospital became our model as we established the Mark & Brenda Moore and Family Foundation to bring some greater clarity and focus to our philanthropic efforts. We try to marry head and heart in each decision—ensuring it is a wise use of the money, while also having some sense of personal connection to the cause. We don't just want to write a check; we want to invest something of ourselves, too.

And it's not just about us. We believe that much of who we are is a result of who our parents were and how they helped shape our lives: that's why it's the "and Family" foundation, in honor of them. We hope that Jenée and Markus will carry the baton in due course, too.

So far through our foundation we have been privileged to give a significant amount of money to twenty different organizations, some large and some small. Some people tell us we are generous, but I tell them that we are not, because it is not our money—it is God's and we are just trying to be sure we use it well for Him.

In addition to financial resources, we also have business skills and connections that can be valuable to organizations. So anything we support involves not just our treasure, but our time and our talents, too—like the numerous fund-raising galas we have hosted. As we are often inviting friends and business associates we know to consider investing in projects, we want to be sure that the projects we are involved with have high standards. I also serve on seven boards, where I get to offer some of my business and leadership experience.

Having formalized our foundation, we identified four areas we wanted to focus our efforts on: healthcare, education, arts and culture, and Christian evangelism. They are, if you will, the cornerstones of what we want to build—not something that is a monument to us, but something that brings life to others, in different ways.

Healthcare is an obvious passion. We know how critical good health is to a fulfilling life, and how easily that can be taken away, in a moment. Even taking the best care of oneself isn't a protection from accident and sickness. And when you are sick, you want to know that you can have access to the best help possible.

In addition to supporting immediate healthcare, whether providing much-needed equipment or helping with development projects like the new hospital tower, we also believe it is important to look to the future. Our giving includes genome research. I wonder whether my strokes might have been avoided, for instance, if there had been simple tests available that revealed my blood deficiency. And might Mom and Michael still be with us had their likelihood of getting cancer been better known?

We are also enthusiastic supporters of EmPowered to Serve, an initiative supported by the American Heart Association and the American Stroke Association to involve churches and other religious groups in promoting heart disease prevention, especially among African Americans and other minority groups, among whom the incidence is disproportionately high. African Americans' risk of stroke is almost twice that of whites, and they are significantly more likely to die as a result. The reasons are complex but include lifestyle and eating habits, where we want to encourage better choices.

Education is a must for us too. We know that neither of us would be where we are today without having benefited from the schooling we enjoyed. I don't believe that everyone has to go to college, but those who have the potential shouldn't be precluded because of lack of money or support.

We are pleased to help the Posse Foundation, where Brenda sits on the advisory board in Washington, DC. It was founded in 1990 by Deborah Bial after a student from a minority background told her he would never have dropped out of college if he'd had his "posse" with him, the friends he had grown up with, rather than being left to figure his transition to college and the wider world on his own.

Deborah's organization now draws together small groups of high school students in multicultural scholarshipped teams that help and encourage one another through their university years. We have also endowed a scholarship program at Antioch that annually supports several students from the church, many of whom we have come to know through our involvement in the youth ministry.

Our interest in culture may surprise some people, but in many ways it is an extension of our commitment to providing educational opportunities. Though I was a math kid, I always appreciated the arts—even if I didn't pull my weight in band class. We believe that history, music, and literature are important in helping form and shape character. People need to be well rounded.

One of the ways we have supported efforts in this area is by becoming founding donors for the National Museum of African American History and Culture, which opened in fall 2016 on the National Mall in Washington, DC, close to the Washington Monument. I can't think of a more fitting location for an institution celebrating and honoring my heritage than near to where Dr. Martin Luther King famously intoned, "I have a dream," in 1963.

We also support the capital's John F. Kennedy Center for the Performing Arts, where I am on the board of directors for the National Symphony Orchestra (NSO). It has been rewarding to be part of efforts to broaden the appreciation of classical music among young people by bringing in unlikely guest artists to perform with the NSO, such as *American Idol* winner Fantasia and rapper Kendrick Lamar.

One unexpected personal bonus from being involved with the NSO came with an invitation for board members to sit alongside the musicians onstage, during a rehearsal. It was a thrill to literally look over their shoulders as they played, admiring how all those hours of practice came out with such seemingly effortless precision and fluidity. And I felt that being there, closely watching their skill and concentration, almost made up for my own lapse back in band class.

The fourth focus of our giving also runs as a thread through the other three—Christian evangelism. Maybe it's because I came to the realization later in my own life, but I believe it's so important for faith to be woven into every aspect of our lives, not just relegated to Sundays. After all, God created us and knows best what we need; He has the answers to any questions we might have, from family and relationships to work and money.

Because the Bible is so full of wisdom, we want to invest in people who can help share it with others. That is how I came to serve on the board of the John Leland Center for Theological Studies, helping prepare church leaders for their preaching and teaching ministry, for example.

I can't emphasize too much the way in which the desire we have for other people to come to know more of Jesus is central to all our philanthropy in its different forms and emphases. You see, some people think I give my money away as a thank-you to God for restoring my life, like I am somehow trying to pay Him back.

Nothing could be further from the truth, though I am of course grateful for what He has done for me. I'm not trying to pay back; I am trying to pay it forward. I want other people to experience the relationship with God I discovered through the experience of my strokes. Knowing His presence is the destination: the strokes were just the vehicle He used to get me there. It might be different for someone else, but what's most important is that they get there too.

Evangelism doesn't just mean telling people about God's love, however; it's also important to demonstrate it—just as Jesus didn't only speak about the kingdom of heaven, but also brought it into people's lives by meeting their physical needs.

That is how Brenda and I found ourselves in Haiti early in 2016, in a former small hotel with no hot water in Jacmel, a coastal town in the south of the country. The building is now Isaiah House, one of the centers through which Community Coalition for Haiti (CCH) provides healthcare, education, and community services in a country that was already ranked one of the poorest in the world, before being further devastated by the terrible earthquake of 2010 and then Hurricane Matthew in 2016.

Brenda and I had been invited by Wayne Reichman to visit and learn more about CCH, founded by two churches in Vienna, Virginia. A vascular surgeon, Reichman had retired from his practice to become the organization's full-time medical director. During our time in Haiti, Brenda got to scrub up and assist in some of the surgeries correcting goiters, which are common because of widespread iodine deficiency. I took part in organizing medical records for some of the patients, and together we helped distribute free reading glasses. The way people's eyes lit up when they were given such a simple, basic aid, you would have thought they had won the lottery.

Equally moving was attending church on Sunday morning, with people so keen to be there that there was already an overflow before the seven a.m. service began, with many sitting outside. Though it was all in Creole, we followed most of what was going on with the help of a translator. Even during the parts we did not understand, there was no mistaking the deep joy in everyone. Though we did not share their language, and our everyday lives were worlds apart, we felt a deep connection through our shared love of Jesus Christ.

It is gratifying to be able to take some of what God has given us and use it to help others in so many different ways. Having some kind of personal connection with the organizations we support—whether that's sitting in with members of the NSO in Washington, DC, or sitting in with surgeons in Jacmel, Haiti—is important to us.

Those kinds of ties also keep taking me back to Jamaica, Queens. I like to get back to visit my old neighborhood, to remind myself how much God has blessed me. Many of the kids I knew back when I was growing up there never left the area. Others did, but sadly not well—they are either dead or in jail.

I have returned to my old schools to speak to some of the classes, recalling my time there and encouraging the students to work hard. The invitations came after I'd written to each of the schools expressing my appreciation for what staff there had invested in me. I asked after Mrs. Wright, hoping that I might be able to track her down personally, but learned that she had retired some years previously, and I was sadly unable to locate her.

When I'm with the students I tell them where I used to live and what I remember of the school, and then I tell them about my career and how much we sold Segovia for. Their eyes get big when they hear that, and then they want to ask all kinds of questions. What kind of car do I drive? Have I ever flown in a jet? I'm happy to answer all their questions. I'm not trying to brag to them, but I want them to think that if I could get to where I am from that school in Jamaica, Queens, maybe they can too. I talk about the importance of working hard, even at their young age. Every choice they make matters, I say. Then I go on to tell them that money isn't the most important thing in the world. Worth more than that, I say, is something that cannot be bought: faith, family, and friends.

I emphasize the same three Fs with the teenage boys I get to mentor through my involvement with Sigma Pi Phi, the African American professional fraternity I was invited to join a few years ago. But I also offer them another three letters for guidance: PHD. When I first say it, they think I'm talking about academic qualifications, but I go on to break it down into essential character qualities they should develop: patience, hard work, discipline.

These are not popular concepts in today's world, which emphasizes the instant. But I explain how they have worked for me, twice over: first when I applied myself to my studies and my work, opening the door to unexpected material success. "You may not be the smartest kid in the class," I tell them. "And you don't have to be. But you can be the hardest-working student in the class; that's within your control." Then I also talk about how PHD worked after my strokes as I applied myself to my recovery, really surrendering to God for the first time in my life, while at the same time doing everything I could to cooperate with Him and His plan.

I make a point of telling these young men about my D grades, too. I want them to know that it is possible to come back from failures, that they should always have hope. A lack of hope, I believe, is at the root of many of our country's problems. When people see no way out of their situation, their despair often drives them to make poor choices—choices that affect themselves and others adversely.

As I have said previously, Brenda and I don't attempt to force our faith on anyone, nor do we use our giving to "buy" the opportunity to talk about God. But we can't separate what we do from what we believe, and if anyone asks, I am always thrilled to have the opportunity to tell them more and try to point them to Jesus. That's simply following what the Bible says in 1 Peter 3:15: "in your hearts honor Christ the Lord as holy, always being prepared to make a defense to anyone who asks you for a reason for the hope that is in you; yet do it with gentleness and respect."

Though faith is so important to me these days, I never want to come across as though I have all the answers. I don't—but, as the saying goes, I know Someone who does. My aim is to more and more live in a manner that is pleasing to God and points others to Him.

I believe that our faith is really measured only by how we change. You simply can't have an encounter with God, like I did, and remain the same.

I'm keenly aware of that for myself as I look back on life BS. I don't believe that I was a hypocrite in my prior life; that's someone who says one thing and does another. I always tried to hold to good moral standards, but I didn't give God His due place in my life. So for me, transformation means continuing to surrender on a daily basis, making time to listen for God's leading instead of relying on my own wisdom. And it means living differently, with a new focus: helping others rather than just getting ahead.

From time to time I get to drive past Mount Vernon Hospital, which I always remember as the place where my second life started. I had surrendered to God while lying immobile in a bed at Reston Hospital, but it was at Mount Vernon that I took my first steps in this new life—literally and figuratively—as I began to learn that letting go of control was ultimately not scary because He is better at being in charge than I am.

I look back on my time in the hospital as being when I had my stroke of faith, not fate; when I encountered God in a new way—and when I also discovered more deeply the richness of family and friends. Each May 12, I take some time to thank God again for His goodness and make a point of connecting with family and special friends to recall what happened and how God brought us through.

It feels a little odd to drive past Mount Vernon and see *Mark and Brenda Moore* high on the wall of the new patient block in big letters; I'm still a private person, by nature. But I believe that we go through things in life that we are meant to share with others.

Dr. John Phillips, my family doctor, tells my story anonymously to other stroke patients he deals with, from time to time, to encourage them. He describes my recovery as "exceptional." One time he told me, "The degree of the recovery you have made is truly remarkable."

Members of the medical community tend to be cautious about their words, naturally, but one nurse who cared for me while I was in my induced coma had no doubt about the magnitude of things. "He is a miracle child," she would tell Brenda whenever she came into my room. "He is a miracle child."

I gratefully agree, though sometimes I forget how far I have come because it is all so close to me. When I speak to support groups where people marvel, I am reminded that my recovery has been amazing. I attribute it in part to the wonderful care I received from so many dedicated professionals and to the unceasing support of my wife, but most importantly to God's loving hand. My hope is that others may turn to Him and find the same to be true for them, that He makes the impossible possible.

If anyone passing Mount Vernon Hospital remembers the names they see high on the wall there, my wish more than anything is that they may be prompted to find out more about our story, and through that be encouraged to look up even higher—to heaven.

STROKE: MY RECOVERY GUIDE

When I first heard the word *stroke*, it sounded like a death sentence to me: life as I had known it was over. But since I was felled by not one stroke but two, I have found that the word can actually point the way to a new and even richer life.

Here are the six things I have discovered to be essential in finding new life following my near-death experiences, spelled out in the word *stroke*.

1. **S is for *starting over.*** You have to start by accepting that life will be different now—but that does not have to mean worse. Wishing it had never happened is a waste of time and energy. Look forward, not behind you!

2. **T is for *target.*** Be sure to focus in on what is going to help you in your recovery. Make faith, family, and friends the three-part foundation on which you build your new life. Keep these priorities clear in your mind.

3. **R is for *receive.*** Be open to all the help and encouragement you can get. Work and cooperate with all who are part of your recovery team, from the healthcare professionals to the personal friends, and draw on the unique contributions each can make to your recovery. Your recovery is a team effort.

4. **O is for *outline.*** Sometimes, when you are in the middle of it all, recovery can seem to be slow in coming. So it can be helpful to set goals to work toward, achievements that

measure your progress, whether that's running a 5k or planning to learn a new hobby or skill. Things like this can be mile markers on the road to the future.

5. **K is for *kneel*.** Humility is essential: others will be able to help you only if you are willing to be vulnerable and open to receiving help, to letting people see you "naked." It's not weak to be weak; in fact, acknowledging weakness can become a source of strength. Above all, I believe, surrendering to God is the gateway to finding His peace and power.

6. **E is for *exert*.** While you can't force recovery through gritted teeth, it's essential to cooperate with the process by investing all you can, from rehab exercises to good diet. So be sure to show up every day and do your part. Give it your best shot—and then leave the rest to God.

AFTERWORD

I first met Mark and Brenda in 2007 when they began attending Antioch Baptist Church in Fairfax Station, Virginia. By then, Mark had been through the worst of his ordeal and was well on the road to recovery from his strokes.

They had been coming to our church for a while when one Sunday the message seemed to grab his attention. It moved him and Brenda to join Antioch as full members. It was as though God had shouted in his ear, "Mark, here's where I want you to serve!" It was as if God had told him that this was not the time for them to be pew warmers; it was time to get off the bench and get in the game. And wow, did they ever!

Many people in churches attend only on Sunday morning, and that is the extent of their commitment to God. If the saying is true that twenty percent of the people in church do eighty percent of the work, then Mark and Brenda are definitely in that twenty percent.

Their approach to serving God reminds me of two people in a three-legged race. If you have ever seen one, you'll know that most people struggle and stumble in taking their first steps tied together. Mark and Brenda are sprinting to the finish line together, full speed ahead! They bring their passion to honor and serve God in all they do.

A very, very accomplished businessman, Mark has bought and sold companies, managed companies, grown companies, and raised millions of dollars to fund companies. He constantly turns down lucrative offers, made because of his significant achievements and business acumen, to reenter the fray of the business world. He has truly left a big footprint in business, but now he is making an even bigger footprint serving God.

Mark not only talks the talk, but also walks the walk. In other words, he is authentic in his faith, which is reflected in his work. Some people come to church for photo ops or because it's considered the appropriate activity in the community. Not Mark: he attends not for show but to worship and serve his God.

Why can I say this? Well, as his pastor I see how he is very generous with the resources God has provided him and Brenda. But it doesn't stop there. They are also active in serving God through their local church and in the larger community. I've seen God stretch Mark and Brenda beyond their comfort zones as they have served without fanfare, not for a photo op, but out of a sense of faithful service to God.

You might ask, Why would they do this? What motivates them? After all, they are at a point in life when they could kick back and just coast to the finish line. In my humble opinion, as I have gotten to know Mark and Brenda, it boils down to their love for God, which compels them to serve wherever He would have them be. Whether it's raising millions of dollars for a local hospital or serving the poorest of the poor, for them it's all about God.

They are so grateful to God for what He has done in their lives. They realize that Mark did not heal himself, but that he owes it all to God. Not that they are denying the great skill of the doctors, the excellent rehab therapists, or the help of their wonderful family and friends, but ultimately they know it was

God who brought him from death's doorway to a renewed and refocused life.

In 2013, I had the privilege of attending and officiating the wedding of Mark and Brenda's daughter, Jenée. I remember how at the rehearsal dinner Mark addressed the gathering of family and friends with eyes filled with tears as he told them how grateful he was to be able to walk his daughter down the aisle, to see that day, because had the events of 2007 gone another way he would not have been around to do so.

Mark is a man who realizes the fragility and brevity of life, that none of us have come to stay. Further, he cherishes each day as a true gift from God. He strives to make the most of each day, because it did not have to be.

I believe that Mark's miraculous recovery is in large part because of his strong faith in God. I believe that God uses all the resources and tools around us. I believe that God gives us the gifts of science and medicine to be used in the care and healing of people. And I believe that faith is the glue that pulls it all together in the healing process.

Faith is what keeps us from giving up when the pain is too great. Faith helps us to press on when we would like to give up in the midst of our illnesses. Faith is a key factor in the healing arts. Mark is very thankful for all that the doctors and care providers do, and he thanks God for them, but it's faith that gets him over the hurdle.

When Mark first shared his story with me, I saw a man who had been through the storm and believed that God had brought him through. He had been knocked down by his strokes and raised up by faith. Mark's healing has not brought him back one hundred percent, physically, but his faith has enabled him to cope. His faith won't allow him to have a pity party. Instead, it enables him to say, "It could have been a lot worse. And I am thankful to be alive."

Mark believes that God kept him alive for a purpose, and he lives it out every day. He loves his wife, his best friend. He adores his wonderful adult children as they make their way in this world. And God has blessed him to see his first grandchild. Mark relishes each and every day and truly uses all that God has given him to be a blessing to others and to point people to Jesus Christ, the source of his faith.

Mark and Brenda do a lot of things anonymously. But God knows, and in God's economy there is a "reaping and sowing" system. Mark and Brenda give so much to so many in so many different venues, so much of it behind the scenes, and God sometimes rewards them openly.

In December 2014, the hospital that tended so wonderfully to Mark's care and recovery named a newly constructed wing after them both in recognition of how they had led the effort with their philanthropic gift and garnered others to do likewise. The Mark and Brenda Moore Patient Tower at the Inova Mount Vernon Hospital is their contribution to ensuring that future patients will continue to receive the high quality of service and care they experienced. It's just one example of their using what God has given them to bless others.

I pray that Mark's transparency in this book has inspired you and encouraged you, either in your current situation or in what you may face in the future. What should you do, having read his story? I recommend that you strive to be a similarly positive influence in your sphere: use whatever God has given you to serve others; pray and ask God to give you the faith to press through whatever life brings; and cherish each day God gives you.

If you can do this, then in the words of the old spiritual, "If I can help somebody, as I travel along...my living shall not be in vain."

Keep the faith.

Rev. Dr. Marshal L. Ausberry, Sr.
Senior Pastor
Antioch Baptist Church
Fairfax Station, Virginia
July 2016

ACKNOWLEDGMENTS

If I learned one thing as a businessman, it's that you can have the greatest idea in the world, but if you don't have people who can help turn that vision into a reality, then it is going to remain unrealized. No one really achieves anything alone.

That has certainly been true for me—twice over. First in building a successful career, and second in rebuilding a life, or, rather, constructing a new one. Simply put, I believe that God puts people in your path to help you, and I'd like to acknowledge some of those He has sent my way.

I'm grateful to all who first sparked in me a love for learning and the belief that education could be my passport to the world. Among them, my early teachers: Mrs. Wright, Mr. Kaufman, Ms. Kelly, and Mrs. McConnell. As I got older, there was Mr. Young and Dr. Paul. I continue to remember them all.

In business, I was fortunate to work for and with men who saw my potential and gave me room to try to grow. Stan Sech opened the first big door for me. Later, Mike Wheeler would become not only my closest business ally, but pretty much another brother. I remain indebted to each of them.

If it takes a village to raise a child, as they say, then it can take a city to save a life. More people than I will ever know had some part in my recovery from near death, and I am forever thankful for the care of so many in the medical and rehabilitation community that came around me. Without Dr. Anje Kim's skilled intervention, there would never have been a chance for recovery; without therapists Stephanie, Lisa, and Sandip's inspiring help, in particular, I would likely not have come as far as I have.

The love of family and friends has been incalculable. My wife Brenda's devotion has been inexhaustible. My daughter, Jenée, and her husband, Gerald, and my son, Markus, have been endlessly supportive. I'm grateful, too, for my siblings—Mike, Greg, Sharon, Joanne, Rochelle, Donna, and Gary—and childhood friend Lenny Richards, for their encouragement and belief in me.

My pastor, Rev. Dr. Marshal L. Ausberry, and the congregation he shepherds at Antioch Baptist Church have been very instrumental in helping me grow in my newfound, post-strokes faith. I am so glad to be part of the church family there.

In being encouraged to share my story with others, I have been helped by Dave Hahn and Sharon Farnell and the rest of the team at Media Connect, who have guided me into what is for me the new world of the media, managing my speaking invitations and opportunities and guiding my social media presence.

I am thankful to Dave Conti, for first working with me to put my story down on paper. Literary agent Bruce Barbour and his wife, author Karen Moore, were Godsends, providing further advice and direction. Andy Butcher, thank you for helping me put my story into words so that people of faith can understand.

In truth, this list really only scratches the surface of all those to whom I owe my thanks. Though I cannot name them all, I am grateful to each one. They are all part of this story.

Mark A. Moore

MacLean, Virginia

August 2016

FURTHER CONTACT

To read more, including my latest news and blog posts, visit my website at AStrokeofFaith.com.

You can follow me on Facebook at www.facebook.com/mark andbrendamoorefamilyfoundation and on Twitter at twitter.com/markmoore325.

To invite me to speak, contact David Hahn at david.hahn@finn partners.com or at 212-593-5847.

Stroke Resources
Organizations

American Stroke Association
http://www.strokeassociation.org
Helpful information on recognition, prevention, treatment, and recovery.

American Heart Association
http://www.heart.org
Research, advice, and news on heart-healthy living.

Books

Forgiven: The Amish School Shooting, a Mother's Love, and a Story of Remarkable Grace by Terri Roberts (Bethany House Publishers): A remarkable account of overcoming bitterness and loss and letting go of the past.

In an Instant: A Family's Journey of Love and Healing by Lee and Bob Woodruff (Random House): An inspiring story of one couple's recovery from a crippling brain injury.

My Stroke of Insight: A Brain Scientist's Personal Journey by Jill Bolte Taylor (Plume): An insightful account of a brain scientist's own recovery from a stroke.

Still Alice by Lisa Genova (Pocket Books): A moving novel about Alzheimer's with real-life takeaway lessons for families facing major health crises.

Wooden: A Lifetime of Observations and Reflections On and Off the Court by John Wooden (McGraw-Hill Education): Lessons in the three-F foundations for a full life: faith, family, and friends.

FINDING FAITH

If reading this book has nudged you to want to know more about God, let me encourage you to follow that prompting—you won't be disappointed! And I have a couple of simple suggestions to help you.

First, go to church! If you've never been, or it has been a long time since you have, know that your impressions or memories of what church is like may well be wrong. The people there are no different from you—except for finding faith in a God who loves them.

They have hopes and dreams and headaches and struggles just like you and me, and if they really know God for themselves, and not just about Him, they will be happy to talk with you.

If, for some reason, you're not able to find a good local church to visit, then come to mine! Services at Antioch Baptist Church are live-streamed each week, and you can join us at http://www.antioch-church.org. You'd be most welcome.

Second, read more about God. There are lots of books written by people like me whose lives have been changed by God, but I suggest that you read His own—the Bible.

Find a version that's easy to read and understand. My translation of choice is the English Standard Version, but there are others you might prefer.

You can read the entire Bible in many different versions online free at https://www.biblegateway.com, or download the free YouVersion app for your phone, which offers multiple translations and reading guides. For more information, go to https://www.youversion.com/apps.

I pray that as you explore, you will find what you are looking for: God does not play hide-and-seek. Indeed, Jesus promised, "Ask, and it will be given to you; seek, and you will find; knock, and it will be opened to you. For everyone who asks receives, and the one who seeks finds, and to the one who knocks it will be opened" (Matthew 7:7–8).

MY TOP TWENTY-FIVE
GOSPEL SONGS

Gospel music played a big part in my recovery, providing the inspiration and drive to keep me going through rehabilitation and training for running my first-ever 5k, almost a year to the day after my strokes.

I know it's also encouraged others, including Aunt Ann. One of my mom's sisters, she had been a big encourager during my recovery, sending messages of love and support. So when I learned she had cancer, I sent her an iPod loaded with some of my favorite gospel music, hoping it would help her as it had helped me.

Though she eventually succumbed to the disease, she remained upbeat throughout, determined to enjoy life to the fullest as long as she was around. I believe that some of the music I shared helped fuel her positive attitude.

I'm not able to send everyone an iPod with inspirational music, but I can share with you my personal Top Twenty-Five Gospel Songs; I hope you might find them an encouragement too. Enjoy the music, which will pump you physically, but be sure to tune in to the words, too, as they will feed you spiritually!

"Center of My Joy"
Richard Smallwood

"Abundantly Blessed"
Ed Montgomery

"Lord I Lift Your Name on High"
Jonathan Butler

"Falling in Love with Jesus"
Jonathan Butler

"He Touched Me"
Traditional

"Total Praise"
Richard Smallwood

"I Know He Cares"
Jonathan Butler

"Worth"
Anthony Brown & Group TherAPy

"Order My Steps"
Traditional

"No Greater Love"
Smokie Norful

"Because of Who You Are"
Vicki Yohe

"If I Believe"
Charlie Wilson

"Your Great Name"
Natalie Grant

"Jesus Is Love"
Smokie Norful

"Expecting Great Things"
Veronica Petrucci

"You Reign"
William Murphy

"It's Working"
William Murphy

"Greatest Man I Know"
VaShawn Mitchell

"Nobody Greater"
VaShawn Mitchell

"Tell Them"
Andrae Crouch

"My Tribute"
Andraé Crouch

"You Alone"
Arkansas Gospel Mass Choir

"Something Happens"
Bishop Paul S. Morton

"Like No Other"
Byron Cage

"Celebration Medley: This the Day…"
West Angeles Church of God in Christ Mass Choir

INDEX